Being the Best You Can Be

A guide on personal development for managers

IAN HUNT

Chandos Publishing
Oxford · England

Published in association with

Institute of Leadership
& Management

Chandos Publishing (Oxford) Limited
Chandos House
5 & 6 Steadys Lane
Stanton Harcourt
Oxford OX29 5RL
UK
Tel: +44 (0) 1865 884447 Fax: +44 (0) 1865 884448
Email: info@chandospublishing.com
www.chandospublishing.com

First published in Great Britain in 2006

ISBN:
1 84334 211 1 (paperback)
1 84334 212 X (hardback)
978 1 84334 211 3 (paperback)
978 1 84334 212 0 (hardback)

© I. Hunt, 2006

British Library Cataloguing-in-Publication Data.
A catalogue record for this book is available from the British Library.

Typeset by Domex e-Data Pvt. Ltd.
Printed in the UK and USA.

Printed in the UK by 4edge Limited - www.4edge.co.uk

Contents

Preface

Could a spare thirty minutes of reading revitalise your ways or working, thinking and living?

I think so.

In this volume I have gathered the best parts of my knowledge of management techniques to provide managers in all walks of life with a reference manual that is also designed as a day-to-day working tool. My aim is to pass on thought processes and skills that will revitalise your way of working, thinking and living.

I have been delivering courses in management techniques for over 12 years to a wide range of businesses and I am always delighted to see the impact they have on people who not only want to improve themselves but also help their people to enjoy their work through effective delegation and motivation skills.

However, when the invitation came to write a book, I hesitated to apply as I have no previous experience as an author. Then I realised that 'writing a book' was one of my 'things that I want to do' and I have had it written down on my 'wish list' for about five years now, so I knew that this was my time.

I have enjoyed the process of distilling my knowledge of management skills and selecting the best nuggets for this book. I hope you enjoy reading it and, as a bonus, benefit by continuing to refer to it whenever your management skills (or your morale) need a boost.

About the author

Ian Hunt is a professionally qualified facilitator with a unique training style that relaxes people and helps them to enjoy the workshops that he runs. His specialist subject is 'motivation' skills and this involves motivating oneself before attempting to motivate others.

Ian works with many public and private companies, across different sectors, and he finds that the subject of People Management is a common requirement for all types of businesses, so feels confident that he can help any type of business with 'people challenges'.

Ian has worked primarily in hospitality, initially in management positions within Thistle Hotels, as Senior Training Advisor with the Hotel & Catering Training Company and latterly as Tourism Training Manager at Scottish Enterprise.

He became self-employed in 1992, and under the trading name of Training Solutions has delivered many management courses, first under the umbrella of the NEBSM (National Examinations Board for Supervisory Management) and now the ILM (Institute of Leadership and Management).

Ian delivers training courses throughout Britain and works closely with a number of Scottish Enterprise Local Enterprise Companies.

In addition to management courses, Ian delivers a number of courses, including Trainer Training (one-to-one skills and group training skills), Customer Service and Assertiveness Techniques.

Ian believes that training and personal development is all about 'energising and enabling positive change'.

The author may be contacted by telephone or e-mail:

Tel.: +44 (0)1382 360098
E-mail: *ian.hunt@tiscali.co.uk*

Introduction

Why do you want to be the best you can?

That's a good question to answer. Well, what is life all about? I have read lots of personal development books and they all seem to point at the same solutions. It is all about balance in your life, the desire for knowledge (on an ongoing basis) and making things happen.

In his book *How to be Brilliant*, Michael Heppell explains that there are eight main areas in your life that you should be considering on a weekly basis: health, close family, money, relationships, contribution, vision, career and personal development. Michael explains that to be a well-rounded individual we should spend enough time on each area so that our life balance stays in check.

This book does not claim to have all the answers to a happy balanced existence; however it is likely that if you consider the options that it covers and explores and then take positive action in some of these areas, you will have a happier and more fulfilled lifestyle.

The following chapter will look at organising yourself, which seems a logical starting point. We have all heard the phrase, 'If you don't know where you are going, then you are unlikely to be successful.' How many people do you know who are very successful and not organised? There will always be some, but normally there will be someone beside them taking up the organisational role.

I feel that it is vital to know what you want and to organise yourself to go for what you want. Don't just think it, but actually do it. How often have you thought, 'I must develop my skills in delegation/PowerPoint skills/marketing etc.'?

How often have you carried that want through and actually done anything about it? The reason for not following through is sometimes due to a lack of focus, a lack of organisation, a perceived lack of time, no energy, lack of prioritisation, etc. The list is endless; we are great at not following through with certain tasks.

Chapter 2 will look at ways of doing the right things at the right time and encourage you to start changing the way you do things as from today. Why not? You gain the benefit from now if you start to change now. Come to think of it, everyone you come into contact with will gain the benefit of your new efficiency, your family, work colleagues, perfect strangers, etc. Everyone wins!

It has been written with your time limits in mind so the subsections are no more than a couple of pages long. Everyone has time to read a few pages at one go.

Organising yourself

Do you have a plan?

If you can dream it, you can do it. (Walt Disney)

If you have a plan then you have a chance of achieving a lot more than if you don't. Do you know exactly where you are going? On waking up each morning, do you have a clear objective for the day? If you do, then doesn't that make you feel great? Do you know what you want to be doing in a year's time, five years' time, ten years' time? Do you have an overall vision for your future?

If you study successful people you will find that the most successful all had (and have) a plan or vision, and they have dedicated their lives to fulfilling that plan. The list of people who have succeeded as a result of a life focus is endless: Mohammad Ali, Richard Branson, Margaret Thatcher, Neil Armstrong, Winston Churchill, Nelson Mandela, Ernest Shackleton, etc.

It is said that Neil Armstrong when he was a small boy told his mother he would walk on the moon when he was older. He told everyone that this was what he was going to do, and as he grew older, he kept this vision clearly in his mind. He studied, worked hard and became a test pilot. After this he grabbed the opportunity of joining the US Space Program. With hard work and focus, he made his own luck and he landed the chance to go to the moon, and eventually he got the unique break of becoming the first person to walk on the moon.

When you have a clear vision, coupled with passion and enthusiasm, then the chances of you achieving your life's desires are greatly increased. Now is the time to write down what you really want for your life? If you write it down, you have a chance. If you don't write it down, it will remain a dream or a wish. Writing it down is the first step to action.

Many people already know what they want from life, e.g. 'to retire and work in my garden'; 'to work at what I do until I die'; 'to pass my business on to my children'; 'to travel the world slowly over the years and enjoy the trip', etc. What do you want to do?

I attended a business seminar a few years ago and for the first time I actually wrote down what I wanted from life. I spent 30 minutes in complete silence (which is rare for most people nowadays unless they are in bed sleeping), and I wrote a list of about 30 different things. I revisited the list a year later and found I had achieved over 50% of my objectives. My conclusion to this exercise is if you know what you want and you take the time to focus on them, great things can happen.

I have read that your subconscious mind is the creator of this phenomenon.

So why don't you try it!

I suggest that you plan to put aside 20 minutes of your valuable time to carry out this exercise. Please list below 20 different goals that you want to achieve. Some will be work related and others will be what you want for yourself and your family: e.g. go on a management course to help you control and develop your people at work, increase your computer skills, start and complete an Open University course, buy a new house, move to Australia, holiday in Mexico, start your own business, expand your company, etc.

1.	11.
2.	12.
3.	13.
4.	14.
5.	15.
6.	16.
7.	17.
8.	18.
9.	19.
10.	20.

Congratulations! If you have written in the spaces above, you have taken the first steps to changing your life forever.

What you now need to do is gain the motivation to follow through with what you want to achieve. And if you look at successful individuals, you will normally find that they tend to adopt similar strategies. These strategies include:

- being able to think beyond normal limiting thinking;
- taking positive action at every opportunity;
- being able to rest and look after yourself properly;
- take action and make things happen.

Making it happen

Thinking beyond your normal limiting thoughts

This is something that people who want to achieve have to do. So you will have to do it too. How many times have you heard people say, 'I would develop the business but I haven't got the time', or 'I want to run more in-house training but I haven't got the skills', or 'I will try and get down to the gym this week if I get around to it'? All of these and similar phrases are said every day.

All of the above phrases are negative 'self-talk'. We speak to ourselves all the time, our so-called 'internal dialogue'. We listen to what we say to ourselves. It's time to eliminate three words from your everyday vocabulary: 'try', 'can't' and 'but', and you will start to notice a difference in the way you feel and the way people react to you.

Positive people are attracted by positive people! So if you find yourself surrounded by negative people, what does this suggest about you, and what are you going to do about it?

Research suggests that when you begin to analyse people's fears and the things they believe are holding them back, most people are held back by fears that are 90% imaginary, i.e. people make false assumptions or use false evidence that prevents action. You and I are no different. How often have we delayed an action because 'I just couldn't be bothered' or 'the time just wasn't right' or 'I'll wait and see', etc.?

Thinking differently takes effort and practice, so don't expect huge changes immediately. Just take one day at a time, and take every opportunity to make changes for the better. Being upbeat and positive is the way forward. It costs nothing and it will make you feel good about yourself and others around you.

Say positive things or don't say anything.

Take positive action

No one achieved anything by just thinking about it. You not only have to think positively, you have to act positively, i.e.

take the action and make the moves required to gain the rewards that ongoing momentum brings. If you take action as your normal course then it becomes a habit. Most habits take little effort (or so it seems). Don't delay, do it today!

Being able to rest and look after yourself

One of the enemies of people in the modern working environment is stress. Stress is all around us, but there are positive actions that we can take to manage stress and turn it to our benefit. Experts claim that without stress, there would be no life. It's our ability to manage stress that counts, and relaxation is one recommendation for doing just that.

When you relax, you allow your brain to become rejuvenated. Relaxation can take the form of sitting alone or lying down for 10/15 minutes during the day, or it can take the form of mild exercise for 20/30 minutes, followed by a 20/30-minute swim, shower or sitting down and relaxing. It can simply be going for a walk in the park for 20/30 minutes. The purpose is to allow your brain to relax and recharge.

Making it happen

You are now focused and relaxed and know what you want; the next and most important factor to help you succeed is to take a chance but realise that you will not always be successful. In other words, go out and do something and don't worry about the results too much. If it works, great! If it doesn't work, great; you've at least learnt something!

When you take action, things begin to happen for you!

Staying on course

> Sometimes you have to stop the world and get off to really change your life. (Anon.)

Your relationship with your work is a lot like any other relationship that has meaning in your life. The only way you are going to feel good about severing that relationship is if you know that you gave it your best effort. Then, if you decide to leave, you can go with peace of mind, knowing you did everything you could to make it work while you were there.

Think before you take action

Perhaps you have concluded that for you, the scales are tipped decidedly towards leaving. Even in this case, give it all you've got before you make a final decision. Make sure you're not being a victim and that you've done everything you can to make it work where you are.

Consider the options where you are

Ask for what you really want. If the job you want doesn't exist, create a new position on the basis of what's wanted, needed and missing, and what matches your talents. If part-time work might be the answer, or working from home 1 day a week, ask for it. Don't leave before asking.

Have the courage to say 'no'

If you are swamped with work and feel 'burned out', have the courage to say 'no' if asked to take on something else. Other people cannot know all you are doing and will continue to give you work until you say 'stop'. If you are single, ask yourself whether the long hours are truly justified or merely a way to avoid confronting time alone. Schedule activities after work, such as a class you have always wanted to take. Pay for it. Then, if someone else asks you to do extra work, look at your calendar and say, 'Sorry, I can't, I'm booked'.

Don't discuss your plans because they might sound unimportant to you at the moment, and you might go back on your promise to yourself. Support your intention to have a life of your own outside work.

Stay long enough to win the prize

Many people leave their job in frustration before reaping any rewards; they then end up feeling unsuccessful. We live in a society addicted to speed and instant solutions and have forgotten that it takes time for many things to happen. I have worked with many people who quit jobs after 1 or 2 years and who left with the feeling that they hadn't accomplished anything. Give yourself long enough.

Take on something new at work that energises you

We all fall into a rut and become bored after a while, especially if we have been working for many years at the same job. We all need new projects, new relationships, and new challenges to keep us energised and growing. It's up to us to seek them out.

Take a sabbatical

Learning can take many different forms. Perhaps you just need a complete break from work that is longer than a holiday to pursue some different interests or simply relax. Why not request either a paid sabbatical or some unpaid leave.

Your initial reaction to this idea may be that other people can do it, but it's impossible for you. You may be thinking, 'I can't afford it', 'My boss wouldn't let me go', 'The company has never done it before', 'Things would fall apart' or 'They'd never agree to it'. You may be right, but you will never know until you ask, and you may be pleasantly surprised.

Part-time work may be the answer

It is true that if you take this route, you will probably be left out of meetings and some exciting assignments, but that may be a great relief because you will be free to focus on the work you like to do. On your days off, you will have precious time to be with your family, pursue hobbies, start a business of your own or write a book. Just be sure to ask for enough money to cover expenses associated with health insurance and days off if these are not covered by the company.

There is no one way to be successful in your work. The most important question is this: where is the best fit for you that will enable you to blossom and fully express your passions, talents, skills and abilities? If you have tried everything and none of your efforts has made a difference, it's time to leave. Be sure you do so with dignity.

Leading the way – making changes

John Jackson of Sketchley, the dry-cleaning company, has undertaken radical changes over many years of work. John has devised a 100-day strategy in how to make changes within a business or company. He divides his approach into three distinct parts.

The first 30 days

- Take a very good look at what is really going on by meeting a large number of managers, shop-floor employees, bankers, investors, customers and suppliers. Keep asking questions, more questions and yet more questions. Double-check all the answers that you receive.

- Take a good look at the strengths and weaknesses of your people at all levels, i.e. directors, managers and supervisors. For each key employee ask the question: 'Are you good enough to achieve the goals you are going to set the company?' If not, can you coach and redirect their talents? If the answer is no to these two questions, start the process of replacement.

- Replace the culture and working standards of the various facets of the organisation.

The second 30 days

- Prepare the strategic plan for the short and long term. State where you want each division/department of the business to be in terms of financial performance, market share, quality standards, customer service and employee relations by the end of the first 12 months.

- Let each section/departmental manager work out a plan to achieve these goals, and agree priorities and resources required to meet the plan.

- At the group monthly meeting, set out clearly your plans for the year ahead. Ensure everyone understands that they have an input into and support the plan.

The next 40 days and onwards

- Clearly communicate to all levels of employees the tasks that lie ahead of them.

- Set up a concise and clear communication process throughout the organisation/business, to keep everyone updated on progress within each area (particularly their own area) and the company overall.

- Bring about culture change. Put the customer first. Get employees to buy into the change process, and feel they are making a contribution and that this is very much appreciated.

Beware of the main obstacles to change

Jackson has identified that there will always be major resistance to changes, the main ones being apathy and speed of response (i.e. slow).

Be systematic

Jackson recommends that by adopting a systematic approach like the 100-day strategy, you have a real chance to take your business forward and be successful, not just you and the company, but the whole team and in particular all the individuals within the team.

Remember the 100-day strategy

- Observe and identify (first 30 days).

- Preparation and selling of the strategic plans and vision for the company (next 30 days).

- Avoid setting standards and expectations too low.

- Set out your stall and make it happen (ongoing) and don't accept second best.

Definition of leadership

Leadership is getting extraordinary performance out of ordinary people. (Sir John Harvey-Jones)

How do you rate yourself?

Take the self-esteem test

Think about the statements tabulated below: test your awareness of your level of self-esteem and see how you rate.

Please rate yourself according to the following scale: 3, often; 2, sometimes; 1, rarely.

I have a tendency to apologise excessively	
I have difficulty maintaining eye contact with some people	
I am comfortable only in a routine	
I am afraid to voice my opinion in the presence of a large group of people	
I feel anxious quite often, especially in unfamiliar situations	
I am uncomfortable with taking on a leadership position	
I consider myself to be a striving perfectionist, but most of what I accomplish is far from perfect	
I often wish I were someone else	
I feel as though I am in constant competition with my peers	
Criticism greatly upsets me	
I aim to please people constantly	
I worry a lot	
I often harbour feelings of hopelessness	
I am unhappy with my physical appearance	
The future scares me	
I often feel as though nothing is in my control	
I tend to exaggerate stories of success and/or boast often	

I look to others for approval and rely on their support	
I trust only a very select few, or no one at all	
I constantly feel as though I have let down those people who care about me	
I am often afraid of rejection	
Total	

(What your score means)

21–35

Good! Although everyone struggles with his or her own personal self-esteem issues, you have a pretty good idea of your self-worth. Look at the areas where you have answered with a 2 or 3 and remember to give yourself a little more credit and encouragement.

36–50

Low self-esteem could be the root of many of your problems. You aren't giving yourself nearly enough credit. In the next part of this material, I give a few helpful tips towards improving self-esteem. Pay close attention. These tips may give you the opportunity to turn your life around.

51 and above

Warning! Low self-esteem can be extremely detrimental to your emotional and psychological well-being. If you scored in this range, you may want to consider seeing your doctor or other professional help. It is important to get to the root of the problem immediately, and perhaps a professional can help you focus on the positive things in your life rather than the negative.

> **Dare yourself to dream and do**
>
> Pick a dream, any dream. Set it as a goal and take steps
> to achieve it. With each little victory, your overall self-esteem
> will grow.

Beating the time thieves

> Things may come to those who wait, but only the
> things left by those who hustle. (Abraham Lincoln)

The extent to which other people waste your time by
keeping you waiting depends on several factors, not all of
which are out of your control. Here are a number of ideas
to help you not waste time by waiting:

- Always confirm your appointment beforehand – this can
  be either a courtesy call or by confirming your
  appointment by e-mail or letter. Confirming on the day is
  especially important where the appointment has been
  made more than a week in advance.

- Organise your appointments to minimise travel time –
  some well-organised business people are quite willing to
  criss-cross the country from one appointment to another.
  This can be the result of confusing being 'busy' with doing
  'business', a mistake that many often make. So long as the
  wheels are turning, they feel there may be no choice but to
  set up meetings in this way. However, some careful
  forward planning can greatly reduce time spent travelling,
  while making it less likely that an unexpected delay on the
  journey will possibly cause you to miss your appointment.

- Although you should arrive in the vicinity of the meeting
  place in plenty of time, do not enter reception until

five minutes before your appointment – this is usually sufficient time to give your name and details of the appointment to the receptionist or security guard, or to find your own way to the relevant office. If you arrive much earlier, you will be sending all the wrong signals. The message of very early arrival is that you are not especially busy and over-eager to do the deal.

- Reduce stress where possible by giving yourself a margin of error – instead of saying: 'I'll see you at 3.30 p.m.' say: 'I'll see you around 3.30 p.m.' This allows you to turn up between five and ten minutes earlier or later without causing offence. Your ability to make such a general appointment does, of course, depend on the nature of the business and relationship with the other person. But in the days of ever increasing traffic congestion and unavoidable delays, many people are prepared to offer latitude. Of course, the mobile phone can also be a great stress reducer, enabling you to telephone ahead and either apologise for the delay or even reschedule the appointment, should some major problem occur.

- On arrival, clearly announce your name and that of the person you have come to see. Then wait at reception until the person you are expecting to see is contacted. In a busy and/or poorly organised reception, it is not unknown for the contact to remain ignorant of your presence in the building.

- While waiting, always keep busy. Do not sit staring into space or reading a newspaper. Not only does this squander precious 'dead time', which could be put to productive purposes, but also sends out the wrong messages to the other party. It suggests you have nothing better to do with your time than wait in reception, diminishing your status in their eyes. Dictate letters, work on calculations, or read reports, memos or cuttings from your folders. Ask the receptionist if you can use the telephone – the request is rarely refused. In that way you not only put the time to good use, you are showing that you are a busy person and a good time-manager.

The six 'Ps' of proactive management technique

How often have you had that feeling that you are not in control of your work? Your work destiny is in the hands of others? Situations and circumstances that crop up during the working day take you away from the main focus of your work, and you never get a chance to catch up?

Well, don't worry! You, like many others, are being 'held hostage' by poor time management practices and poor personal management practices. What you need to do is to take control of your working life! Here are a number of practical ideas and methods that you can introduce into your working routine immediately:

- Have a work-plan before you start work – write this plan the day before (last thing).
- Don't procrastinate (keep to the most important jobs ... and do them now).
- Don't allow yourself to be distracted; try and keep your work-space clear (tidy and quiet).
- Don't allow yourself to be disturbed (train your colleagues to screen visitors and telephone callers).
- Keep all meetings and telephone calls brief and to the point (don't waffle and don't allow people to waffle to you).

- Allow yourself planning time every day (first thing in the morning and last thing at night). This helps you to focus on the priorities.
- Be assertive: respect other people's time but at the same time protect your limited time.
- As a manager, train your team members to manage their time better (it will make them more efficient and confident and you will have more time-conscious team members).

Always remember the six 'Ps' of proactive management technique: proper preparation and planning prevents poor performance.

How to avoid hitting the icebergs!

As the stern of the *Titanic* lifted out of the water, the crew and passengers struggled with the lifeboats. There were no drills, no rehearsals and most of the crew members were unfamiliar with their responsibilities. The lifeboats were improperly loaded and only one lifeboat went back to recover survivors even though some were less than half full. The real-life tragedy of the *Titanic* teaches us some hard lessons in poor management practice.

Leadership looks below the surface – the greatest danger, as well as the greatest opportunities, lie below. The North Atlantic in 1912 was like glass, deceptively dangerous. The largest part of the iceberg lies below ... unseen. Like steel fangs, it tore at the rivets along the 300 feet of the *Titanic's* hull. Those below (the crew and steerage) felt and saw the damage first. Like a grasping breath, the steam bellowed as chaos reigned below. And now, just like then, those who know what is wrong with the 'ship' are those below.

Furthermore, those below usually have the best ideas and solutions to your problems.

Morals

- Start looking towards your front-line team members for ideas, problems and solutions.
- Ask for the problems to be identified, but don't accept them unless your team members can come up with some practical ideas to overcome them. Do this before you 'hit the icebergs'.
- The best leaders are training their team members (all the time).

None of us was alive when the *Titanic* sank, but we can learn from any mistakes made and we can chart our course in the right direction – let's learn from their mistakes and ensure that we avoid our own *Titanics*.

How to get your point across in 30 seconds

In Milo Frank's book with the title above, he explains that it pays to remember the three 'Ks' of communication: katch them, keep them and konvince them. You catch them with a hook, and then you have to keep them and convince them.

The subject of your 30-second message must explain, reinforce and prove the point you are there to make. In order to do this, the subject must contain all or any part of the famous formula: what, who, where, when, why and how.

Developing your subject

Part One – Know your objective, know your listener and know your approach.

Part Two – Ask yourself the following questions:

- What am I talking about?
- Who is involved?
- Where is it?
- When is it?
- Why is it?
- How do I do it?

Part Three – Check your answers against the following questions:

- Do they reinforce and/or explain my objective?
- Do they relate to my listener?
- Do they correspond to my approach?

Below is an example of a 30-second message.

Making an impact

A managing director who was seeking potential investment in his company said the following to possible investors, 'Can our shares double in value over the next three years? I believe they can and will'. He then went on to talk about his approach. 'We're in the fast-growth business, 2004 proved that. It was the best year in our company's history, record revenues and record earnings. We now have a dominant and growing market share in Europe. We're in the "make you happy" business with a product to match that market. Our advance sales are already setting new records.

Buy our shares now and participate. I did and I am going to buy a lot more.'

The MD told his listeners what he was talking about, where it was, when it was taking place, how it was progressing and why they should buy. Here is another 30-second message.

Making an impact

A doctor who was a medical advisor to a company was talking to one of the company's managers. He started, 'How would you like to die young at a very old age? Preventative medicine is the answer. Did you know that a heart attack is just your heart getting angry with you? You can keep that from happening by treating your heart well and keeping it happy. All you have to do is exercise regularly, don't smoke, avoid fatty foods, and give yourself a totally relaxed day at least once a week. Do these simple things and your body won't get angry with you. I want you to stay healthy, so don't just come to me when you are sick. Call me tomorrow after I have had a chance to look at your results. We can decide if you need to come back next Tuesday to discuss diet and exercise.'

The doctor knew his objective, his listener and his approach. He told the manager what he was talking about – preventative medicine. He then went on to tell him who was involved, and where, why, when and how to stay healthy. He covered all the suggested ingredients that make up the subject of the 30-second message.

Keep to a planned structure

Remember that you need a hook sentence first, then some real substance to follow when you are planning your 30-second message. Your subject is the news story that follows a dramatic headline, the caption under an eye-catching photograph, the chocolates in the attractive box. What, who, where, when, why and how are all part of your subject. It's an easy formula to use, and once you have mastered it, it will pay dividends in every 30-second message.

Writing a personal mission statement

An effective way to help you achieve is to begin with the end in mind. Some people use a personal mission statement or philosophy or creed. It focuses on what you want to be (character) and to do (contributions and achievements) and on the values or principles upon which being and doing are based. As everyone is unique, a personal mission statement will reflect that uniqueness, both in content and in form. Here is an example of a personal creed:

- succeed at home first;
- seek and merit divine help;
- never compromise on honesty;
- remember the people involved;
- hear both sides before judging;
- obtain counsel from others;
- defend those who are absent;
- be sincere but decisive;
- develop one new proficiency every year;
- plan tomorrow's work today;
- hustle while you wait;
- maintain a sense of humour;
- be orderly in person and in work;

- do not fear mistakes – fear only the absence of creative, constructive and corrective responses to mistakes;
- facilitate the success of others;
- listen twice as much as you speak;
- concentrate all abilities and efforts on the task at hand, not worrying about the next job or promotion.

A woman seeking to balance family and work values expressed her personal mission statement differently:

- I will seek to balance career and family as best I can because both are important to me. My home will be a place where I and my family, friends and guests will find joy, comfort, peace and happiness. I will seek to create a clean and orderly environment, yet one that is liveable and comfortable.
- I will exercise wisdom in what I choose to eat, read, see and do at home. I especially want to teach my children to love, learn, laugh and work, and also to develop their unique talents.
- I value the rights, freedoms and responsibilities of our democratic society. I will be a concerned and informed citizen, involved in the political process to ensure my voice is heard and my vote is counted.
- I will be a self-starting individual who exercises initiative in accomplishing my life's goals. I will act on situations and opportunities, rather than be acted upon.
- I will always keep myself free from addictive and destructive habits. I will develop habits that free me from old labels and limits, and expand my capabilities and choices.
- My money will be my servant, not my master. I will see financial independence over time. My wants will be subject to my needs and my means.

- Except for long-term home and car loans, I will seek to keep myself free from consumer debt. I will spend less than I earn and regularly save or invest part of my income.

- I will use what money and talents I have to make my life more enjoyable for others through service and charitable giving.

Once you have a sense of mission, you have the essence of your own proactivity. You have a vision and the values that can direct your life. You have the basic direction from which to set your long- and short-term goals. You have the power of a written constitution based on correct principles, against which every decision concerning the most effective use of your time, your talents and your energies can be effectively measured.

Twenty ways to save time on the telephone

Here are 20 ways to prevent phone bandits from stealing your time.

1. Limit social conversation – avoid time-wasting and irrelevant discussions. Without being discourteous, come swiftly to the point if you have initiated the call, and prevent somebody who has called you from straying too far off track.

2. Provide short answers to questions – do not feel tempted to elaborate needlessly. Say what you have to say and then end the call.

3. Make sure that the key part of your message is clearly remembered – when giving complicated information

over the telephone, start with a brief summary of the message, follow that by repeating it in greater detail and conclude by briefly reviewing the facts.

4. Delegate the taking of calls whenever possible and appropriate.

5. To avoid being disturbed by calls, do work that demands intense concentration earlier in the day – where possible do this work in a room that doesn't have a telephone.

6. Refuse to take calls between certain times – between these times all calls can be delegated or held.

7. Anxiety aroused by difficult calls can waste time – you may delay such a call, even if the matter is urgent and must be resolved quickly. It is better to take time out, relax, go for a walk for 10 minutes outside, and then come back refreshed to deal with a difficult call.

8. Encourage co-operation by using the phrase, 'Will that be all right?' – research reveals that it usually prompts a positive reply from the caller and brings them back into the conversation, and it is more likely that the call will end successfully.

9. Take the initiative and call the person you need to speak to – the advantages are that you get the information when you need it, and it allows you to finish the call within a planned time-frame.

10. Before dialling, always have a clear idea of what you want to achieve – if you are trying to fix an appointment, then if you suggest a time and place, your request will focus the other person's mind on whether he or she can see you, rather than whether he or she really wants to see you.

11. Always start the conversation with 'Good morning/afternoon ...' This gives the other person time to tune in

to your voice, and switch concentration from their previous task to that of dealing with your call.

12. Calling at an inappropriate moment is a major time-waster – the worst time to call is first thing in the morning, when the other person is catching up with mail, dictating letters, planning their day and generally getting their day under way. Always ask, 'Is this a good time to talk briefly, or should I call back?'

13. Telephoning while standing up sharpens the mind – you are more alert and attentive.

14. Listening is a skill that must be learned, practised and perfected before it can be used successfully. Our brain understands speech much faster than we can talk, so our concentration can often drift. Use filler phrases to show that you are listening, e.g. 'mmmm', 'I see your point', 'so what you are saying is ...'.

15. Always listen positively when phoning – this involves not only listening to what is being said but also to what is not being said.

16. Disraeli once said there is 'no index of character so sure as the voice' – as you listen allow the impression of the speaker to form slowly in your mind. These unforced impressions are often remarkably accurate, e.g. fast-paced speech usually means the person you are speaking to is thinking quickly, so speeding up your own speech is possible without any real risk of confusion, and will help build rapport with the person. Hesitations, stammering or pauses indicate that perhaps giving information slowly and confirming things in writing might be best.

17. People like to be communicated to in certain ways – so change your style to suit them. For example,

'Commanders' use language of achievement, such as 'setting goals', moving forward', etc. Be direct and to the point with 'Commanders'; stress how you can help them attain goals or make their time more efficient. 'Comforters' are people who prefer to talk about emotions, e.g. 'my feeling is ...', 'my hunch is ...', 'my gut reaction is ...'. Be prepared to spend a little more time with 'comforters', ask about their health, how their children are, and listen to their ideas or problems. 'Dynamos' use words that convey energy and enthusiasm: 'great', 'this is a really exciting prospect', 'you'll love this', etc. 'Dynamos' speak quickly, urgently, and have lots of ideas. Speak back to them in a lively and enthusiastic manner that conveys a sense of urgency and excitement.

18. A universal rule of human relationships is to have a positive and sincere interest in the other person, and take note of what they say.

19. Get the best out of answering-machines – leave brief and understandable messages, and learn the telephone code (i.e. A – alpha, B – bravo, C – Charlie, etc.) so that you can leave clear and concise messages.

20. End your calls efficiently – chatter on too long and you risk confusing or irritating the other person. Be polite, be firm and be gone. Replace the receiver and start thinking about the next call you want to make.

It's your life – so take charge and develop yourself

Remember: it's your life, and you're in charge

You may decide to develop yourself. Here are ten qualities of self-development.

Courage is the most important of these qualities, and provides the foundation for all the others. There are opportunities every day at work to demonstrate courage. For one person, it might take courage to voice a dissenting opinion or to speak up in a meeting. For another, it might take courage to try something new. It takes courage to question whether our work is a good fit and we are in the right place, to listen to our heart and then to take action.

Empathy is a major skill that we need to develop to cultivate good relationships. It includes the art of listening – listening for, to and with. We must listen for other people's commitments, concerns and enthusiasms; listen to what people are saying on the surface as well as to the music underneath; listen with full attention, separate our thoughts away from our own agenda, and with feeling for other people's position, experience and perspective. It allows people to give us feedback, coaching and ideas (without which we will fail). Learn to listen to input from everyone. This includes listening to yourself and honouring your own needs.

Commitment is about not giving up. We can allow ourselves to be stopped by other people's negative comments; we get hurt; we get discouraged; we lose confidence in ourselves or our ideas; we become overwhelmed by obstacles; we get side-tracked by diversions; we become cynical and give up on our hopes and visions. People who demonstrate commitment are those who are successful; those who give up, are not. Decide what you are committed to and then stick to it, but be clear about the distinction between commitment and attachment.

Openness. When we have invested time and energy in learning a certain way of doing something, it is often difficult to be open to an alternative. We become enthralled with our ideas and turn them into cherished beliefs. But the world is changing rapidly and dramatically, and we will not survive the changes if we are rigid. We can hold on to our standards while letting go old ideas or ways of doing things. With diversity of age, background, culture and gender becoming the norm rather than the exception in the workplace, it is even more important for us to open our minds as well as our hearts.

Responsibility. Taking responsibility for the good stuff is easy. Taking it for the bad is hard, but it's a powerful stand to take and will enable you to move out of the role of victim. It requires a major shift from pointing fingers and blaming everyone and everything else for your circumstances, to 'owning' the situation you are currently in, no matter how it looks. Ask yourself this: given the circumstances, what do I need to do now?

Flexibility. When you begin pursuing your dreams, you can count on meeting obstacles, confronting unexpected developments and finding that some things do not turn out the way you imagined. Flexibility is a quality that will help you continue on your path without giving up your dream. You may, however, have to give up your expectations of exactly how your dream should develop and relax into another version of it. It is important to remind yourself that there are lots of ways to get there, not just one.

Authenticity. Do you put on a 'work face' or assume a work persona when you go to work? If so, I guarantee that what you present at work is not the most alive or interesting to you. The authentic you is far more interesting and vital. Putting on a 'work face' is part of the reason for the trance-like state most people enter into at work. We know when people are not being sincere. It pays to bring the full *you* to work.

Integrity. We all have an internal alarm system that lets us know when we are not acting with integrity. It's our job to listen to this alarm and honour it. Being out of touch with our integrity is like being out of sorts. Something is missing. Our outside actions don't match our inside intentions. Acting with integrity allows us to experience wholeness and completeness.

Resourcefulness. It is common when we are employed by a company to think that someone else will or should provide all the resources we need to be successful in our job. The problem with this attitude is that it encourages us to operate from a sense of entitlement that leaves us passive and dependent. Resourcefulness is like a muscle: use it or lose it.

Generativity. Most people are good implementers. However, you also have to be a generator to be successful at work. A generator creates something out of nothing, makes things happen, takes on new tasks with vigour and keeps things going.

Important things in your life

In Paul McKenna's book *Change Your Life in 7 Days* he asks the question, 'What would you do if the world was going to end one week from today?' He explains that your answer to this is the key to identifying your values – those things that matter to you most in your life. When Paul asked a number of elderly people who were nearing the end of their lives what they wished they had done more of and less of, none of them said, 'I wish I had another Mercedes'. They said things such as, 'I wish I had laughed more and loved more', or 'I wish I had spent less time worrying'.

The opportunities for us to live more abundantly are all around us, but just acquiring the symbols of success will not make us any happier. When you learn to focus on your values and your life's purpose instead of just your goals, you will automatically begin to take the big picture of your life into account.

In the book *The Power of Full Engagement* corporate coach Dr James Loehr offers the following questions to help you get in touch with your core values – the most important things in your life.

Step 1

1. Jump ahead to the end of your life. What are the three most important lessons you have learned and why are they so critical?

2. Think of someone you respect deeply. Describe three qualities in this person that you most admire.

3. Who are you at your best?

4. What one-sentence inscription would you like to see on your tombstone that would capture who you really were in your life?

By looking at the answers to the four questions above, you can decide the most important values in your life.

Step 2

Once you have decided your values, you need to write down what you want in your life. Sit down and write a list. You need to think beyond the possible. George Bernard Shaw once said, 'The reasonable man adapts himself to the world; the unreasonable man persists in trying to adapt the world to himself. Therefore, all progress depends on the unreasonable man.'

Step 3

Only you know what you want out of life: what makes your heart beat faster, what makes you sing? Answer the next few questions; don't stop to consider whether something is possible or not, just let your answers flow ...

- What do you love to do so much that you'd pay to do it?
- What do you really feel passionate about?
- What would you choose to do if you had unlimited resources?
- Who are the people or characters from history you most admire, and why?

Answering these questions will help you to get an overall idea of what your life's purpose is all about. It allows you to expand the limitations of your present mindset and become creative. If you require clarity, McKenna says to ask these follow-up questions:

- What did you want as a child?
- What did you want to be when you grew up?
- What would you do if you were guaranteed success?

I recommend that by asking yourself these sorts of questions, it helps you to decide the way forward based on your thinking when you were younger.

The upward spiral – developing yourself

Renewal is the principle – and the process – that empowers us to move on an upward spiral of growth and change, one of continuous improvement. To make meaningful and consistent progress along the spiral, we need to consider another aspect of renewal, our conscience. In the words of Madame de Stael, 'The voice of conscience is so delicate that it is easy to stifle it: but it is also so clear that it is impossible to mistake it.'

Conscience is the endowment that senses our congruence or disparity with correct principles and lifts us toward them – when it's in shape.

Training and educating the conscience requires concentration, discipline and honest living. It requires regular feasting on inspiring literature, thinking noble thoughts and, above all, living in harmony with its still small voice.

Just as junk food and lack of exercise can ruin an athlete's condition, those things that are obscene or crude can breed an inner darkness that numbs our highest sensibilities and substitutes the social conscience of 'will I be found out?' for the natural or divine conscience of 'what is right and wrong?'

Once we are self-aware, we must choose purposes and principles to live by; otherwise the vacuum will be filled, and we will lose our self-awareness and become like grovelling animals that live primarily for survival and propagation. People who live on that level aren't living; they are 'being lived'. They are reacting, unaware of the unique endowments that lie dormant and undeveloped within themselves. And there are no shortcuts in developing them. The law of the harvest governs: we will always reap what we sow – no more, no less. The law of justice is immutable, and the closer we align ourselves to the correct principles, the better our judgement will be about how the world operates and the more accurate our paradigms – our maps of the territory – will be.

As we grow and develop on this upward spiral, we must show diligence in the process of renewal by educating and obeying our conscience. An increasingly educated conscience will propel us along the path of personal freedom, security, wisdom and power.

Moving along the upward spiral requires us to *learn, commit* and *do* on increasingly higher planes. We deceive ourselves if we think that any one of these is sufficient. To keep progressing, we must learn, commit and do – learn, commit and do – and learn, commit and do again.

Here are some ideas to help apply the renewal principle:

- Make a list of activities that would help you keep in good physical condition, that would fit your lifestyle and that you could enjoy over time.

- Select one of the activities and list it as a goal in your personal diary for the coming week. At the end of the week, evaluate performance. If you didn't make your goal, was it because you overlooked it for a higher value? Or did you fail to act with integrity with your values?

- Make a similar list of renewing activities in your spiritual and mental dimensions. In your social–emotional area, list relationships you would like to improve or specific circumstances that would bring greater overall effectiveness. Select one item in each area to list as a goal for the week. Implement and evaluate.

- Commit to write down specific 'sharpen-the-saw' activities in all four dimensions every week, to do them, and to evaluate your performance and results.

3

Being positive about yourself

Dealing with self-esteem

What is self-esteem?

Self-esteem is the value you place on yourself. Self-esteem encompasses your identity, independence, intimacy, trust, intelligence, competence, talents and confidence. The level you have reached with each of these items will determine whether your self-esteem is high or low.

- Your identity is who you are – your physical, mental, and emotional qualities and characteristics. If you think you are the same as everyone else, then think again and dig deeper. Keep in mind that identity equates to individuality.

- Independence is how comfortable you feel with being in control of your life – decisions, actions, thoughts and feelings. These are all within your power; but do you take control or do you share control among the different factors in your life?

- Intimacy involves the connections we make with others. There are different levels of intimacy and the degree to which you are at ease with these connections can limit your relations. Are you comfortable with intimacy or do you shy away from it?

- Trust is our belief in others. For some, this must be earned after extensive testing; for others, it is given away freely. Your ability to trust others may stem from life experiences or your own securities or insecurities. Do you feel you make good judgement calls? Do you trust yourself to trust others?

- Intelligence is not just knowledge. It also includes common sense and reason. Everyone has intelligence, but some choose to display it more than others. You can always gain more knowledge, but do you take advantage of that? Do you shelter your intelligence, or do you employ it on a regular basis?

- Competence is your ability to respond effectively. Everyone has a set of skills and abilities that can be used to accomplish a feat. However, little can be accomplished until you exercise these skills to the best of your ability. Can others rely on you to complete a task effectively? Can you rely on yourself?

- Talents are those gifts that you were born with. Everyone has them, though many do not take the time to discover or exploit them. Can you name your talents? Or are you convinced you have none?

- Confidence is your belief in yourself and your abilities. Without confidence in yourself, you will never be able to make the most of your skills and talents. You will miss out on opportunities and experiences. Do you have the confidence you need to be the best you can be?

Improve your self-esteem

Try out the following suggestions. You might just have some fun along the way.

- Learn to forgive yourself.
- Surround yourself with stable, happy people.
- Trust yourself.
- Set realistic goals.
- Reward yourself.
- Learn the decision-making process and incorporate it into everyday life.
- Take care of yourself: eat healthy foods, sleep well and exercise regularly.
- Consider your mistakes as tools for learning.
- Take some risks: leave your comfort zone from time to time.
- Focus on your positive attributes.
- Don't rely on the opinion of others: focus on your own priorities, goals, dreams and values.
- Learn to laugh at yourself.
- Above all, you must accept yourself. This means accepting everything about you: your appearance, beliefs, strengths, weaknesses, values, talents, faults, standards, etc.

Positive self-talk

Do you ever pay attention to what you tell yourself, either aloud or inside your head? Well start. Perhaps you have problems with low self-esteem, and consequently time management, because you speak negatively to yourself. Some people don't even realise they are doing it. It is important to take notice of this. Are the words 'I can't' a stable in your vocabulary? What other negative statements do you make about yourself? Be honest. We all do it, and these statements will bring us down. Every time you catch yourself making a negative statement, say the opposite. For instance, if you tell yourself you cannot make a speech in front of a group of people, flip the statement around. Tell yourself that you can make a speech in front of a group of people. Say it aloud. Say it several times. Believe it! Repeat the positive. Set a goal to say a minimum of three (or more) positive statements throughout the day, *every day*.

> To avoid criticism, do nothing, say nothing, be nothing. (Elbert Hubbard, author of *A Message to Garcia*)

Motivating yourself

Motivation takes several factors into consideration. It depends on the type of task that needs to be done, your attitude toward this task, any past experiences you've had with a similar task, your physical health, your stress level, the importance or urgency of the task, and your overall mood. All these factors will influence your level of motivation.

You are in control

It may seem that you have no control over your motivation. People often believe motivation is derived only from outside forces. Although this may be true in some cases, often personal inspiration, or lack of it, has the greatest effect. Either you are motivated or you are not. It's not in your hands: correct?

No. You can take action to help yourself find inspiration for the completion of even the most menial tasks. It will take determination and effort on your part, but what doesn't?

Taking control

Think about the upcoming task. If you aren't looking forward to it, then the problem is right there. What associations do you make with the task? Is it something that brought you displeasure in the past? Do you expect an unfavourable outcome? Does your mind conjure up a thousand more enjoyable things that you could do instead? Are you unsure of your ability to complete the task correctly?

Take action now

Once you know the root of the problem, it is time to take action to dispel negative thoughts. The best way is just to start. Even if you don't know what you are doing, if you just do something, anything that is relevant to the task, the movement itself will serve as a motivator. If you just can't motivate yourself to start a paperwork backlog, for example, force yourself to take the first step. The next step will be easier to take. Once you begin the task and see some progress, you will be more willing to continue and go a little further. Taking a step forward and actually involving physical action will get your blood pumping, and motivation won't be far behind.

Rewards

Another trick is to place a reward at the finishing line. Rewards will tempt you to get started and follow through. Before you start the task, set guidelines for yourself. Be specific about what you want to accomplish and within what period of time. Set up a fitting reward to be granted only on completion. By setting your sights on something that will bring you pleasure, it is easier to overcome any obstacle that gets in your way.

Excuses waste time

Making excuses can tie up your time for no reason. On the next occasion you catch yourself making an excuse, try to calculate just how much time it is costing you. Try and break the habit. You know what you have to do and whether or not you are going to do it. Don't spend time looking for ways out, especially when you know you aren't even going to take them.

Parkinson's Law

Parkinson's Law states that work expands to fill the time allotted for it. In other words, if you give yourself an hour to clean the car, it will take you an hour. If you give yourself two hours, you will do the same work in two hours. Note the following.

- This principle can damage your schedule. If you block out too much time for an activity, you will use all that time to complete it. However, if a lesser time had been allocated, you most likely would have completed the task.

- Parkinson's Law can cause you to give greater importance to activities that really have little value. For example, if you allow a large amount of time to wash the car, you will use all that time to do so, although you could easily run it through a car wash in just a few minutes. You then decide to wax and vacuum the car as well. All the detailing is unnecessary, especially when placed alongside other important activities you could have accomplished within the same time.

- It can also trigger your tendency to procrastinate. If you realise that the same amount of work can be done in half the time, you may put off beginning the project until you are right upon its deadline.

Rewards – some guidelines to consider

- The reward should not exceed the activity in terms of proportion
- A reward should not conflict with a to-do, i.e. you cannot reward yourself by procrastinating or eliminating an item on your to-do list.
- A reward should not conflict with any goals you have set, e.g. do not reward yourself with a double portion of chocolate gateaux if your goal is to lose weight.

A reward must be carried out or delivered within a reasonable time following the completion of the activity. A reward does not work if it does not reflect upon the task completed.

Do you believe in luck?

The Luck Project was originally conceived to explore scientifically the psychological differences between people who considered themselves exceptionally lucky and unlucky. The initial work was funded by the Leverhulme Trust and undertaken by Prof. Richard Wiseman in collaboration with Drs Matthew Smith and Peter Harris. Prof. Wiseman, a scientific researcher looking at unusual areas of psychology, has since built upon this initial work by identifying the four basic principles used by lucky people to create good fortune in their lives. These techniques appear to enhance people's good luck.

This research has involved working with hundreds of exceptionally lucky and unlucky people, and has employed various methods – including psychometric questionnaires, laboratory experiments and intensive interviewing – to understand better the psychology of luck.

The results of this work reveal that people are not born lucky. Instead, lucky people are, without realising it, using four basic principles to create good fortune in their lives.

Principle one: maximise chance opportunities

Lucky people are skilled at creating, noticing and acting upon chance opportunities. They do this in various ways, including networking, adopting a relaxed attitude to life and by being open to new experiences.

Principle two: listening to lucky hunches

Lucky people make effective decisions by listening to their intuition and gut feelings. In addition, they take steps to boost their intuitive abilities actively by, for example, meditating and clearing their mind of other thoughts.

Principle three: expect good fortune

Lucky people are certain that the future is going to be full of good fortune. These expectations become self-fulfilling prophecies by helping lucky people persist in the face of failure, and by shaping their interactions with others in a positive way.

Principle four: turn bad luck to good

Lucky people employ various psychological techniques to cope with any ill fortune that comes their way. For example, they spontaneously imagine that things could have been worse, and do not dwell on ill fortune and take control of the situation.

There is always something to smile about

In a perfect world we'd all be perfect and there would be nothing to moan about, nothing to grumble about and nothing to criticise. As it stands, it is not (yet) a perfect world, things will go wrong, and there will be foul-ups, mistakes and blunders. So expect moaners, groaners and critics. Constructive criticism, delivered with sincerity and in the spirit of doing things better, is no bad thing. If you make a mistake, then best to admit it, offer to put it right and agree a course of action to make sure it doesn't happen again. If you have a grizzly boss and you know there has been a foul-up, the best thing to do is to get in first. Be proactive and confess:

> I'm not really sure how this has happened, and we'll have to look into it to find out, but the Council's account is late on delivery. May I suggest we take the following action to put it right, look into how it happened and make some arrangements to ensure that this type of thing is not overlooked again. I'm really sorry.

This may not save you from getting a roasting but it could save your job.

Cold water torture

Sometimes it may be your colleagues who criticise your ideas. Try and get them onside by speaking to them in private. You'll get to know the kind of thing that makes them become negative: think about it and add it to the equation. Work around the negativity. Negative people are often insecure and lack invention and creativity. In the face of inventive or creative people they feel their own limitations and try to make up for the difference by trampling over your and other people's ideas. Try sharing your ideas with them. Get them onside by offering co-ownership of a project you want to see through.

Try building alliances

Discuss your ideas with colleagues and ask for opinions. Get friends onside and gain positive feedback, before involving any 'grumpy' colleagues. Be sure to reveal your idea when your supporters are present. The dissenters often disappear when they find they have no allies. Sometimes it is a good idea to give away the credit for one of your ideas, just to get it off the ground. Praise for someone else might be just enough to make your idea work.

Words you don't want to hear

'*Nothing like that can be done*' – if you hear these words then try 'I'm sorry to hear that. Tell me why you say that? How can you be sure this particular plan won't work?'

'*We tried it before and got into a real mess*' – 'Yes I know. I looked at the project you are referring to and we will have to be careful to avoid the pitfalls that occurred in the past. Let me explain how this is different.'

'Why do we have to bother with all that?' – 'This approach saves money/time/effort/serves our customers faster [sell the benefits]. Let me explain how ...'

'We don't do things like that here'. – 'I know we don't, but I think we should start. Let me explain why.'

When critics shoot themselves

Criticism is contagious. If the criticism is well founded, don't be precious, take it on board and deal with it, and let everyone know you've done so. Otherwise try to get your main critic on board. 'George, I know that you have strong opinions on this, so before I go public I want to have your views.' Approaching criticism in this way gives you two chances. First, you'll know what the arguments will be and you can prepare. Second, you might end up with an ally. Staff with little confidence will often be self-critical. They seem to think it's easier if they criticise themselves before someone else does. If you are the boss and you have such staff, you must act. Staff are any business's most important asset. It is vital they are motivated, confident and encouraged. Take them to one side and say: 'It is a shame to hear you talking like that. You have excellent skills/experience/energy/enthusiasm/loyalty ... and I hate to hear you waste it. You are doing a good job. See, I've told you. Now tell yourself.'

Think about this

Staff put themselves down in the hope that someone will come along and tell them how great they are at their job.

Don't be sucked into this. Stick with, 'I think we both know what sort of job we're doing. If I didn't think you were good enough, you wouldn't be in the department/team, so let's stick to the facts.'

Change yourself

The environment at Rochester Ford Toyota has changed in recent years. Rob Gregory, the boss, has instigated many changes in the car dealership. Rob loves quick fixes. 'It's part of our nature as a human being. I want what I want when I want it,' he says. 'One of my frustrations is that I think I have this gift: I can see what's wrong with everyone else. But if you want to change the world, first you have to change yourself. That has been very humbling, because I realised that nine out of ten problems in my business have been caused by me. Now I see that. So as I work on myself, I find I have a greater impact than when I was trying to work on other people.'

So Rob worked on himself. He began to learn to listen. 'There are times when Rob doesn't like what you have to say about how he's handled a situation or talked to someone, but he will reflect on it, come back, and be sincerely appreciative,' says Al Utesch, Parts Manager. He began to learn to give his employees freedom. 'Deep down, if I'm honest with myself, I know I still measure things by money,' Rob notes. 'So when people make decisions that have financial repercussions, it's difficult for me not to shoot the messenger or fire at will. However, we have a sign and card with our values noted on them, and they say, "We have nothing of greater value than our people". So what does that look like in practice? Would you be patient while employees learned if you truly valued people? The answer is, "Of course".'

Rob also learned increasingly to be led by the business's vision, not short-term considerations. 'One of our customers called us up,' he recalls. 'He's going out to Idaho. The truck he bought from us is acting up in a blizzard in South Dakota. He's at another dealership and he says they can't fix it today. I said, "If they can't, pick a vehicle from their lot, load your stuff into it, and I'll buy it from them for you when you get back." Well the dealer fixed the truck; I think they saw how committed we were and their pride got involved. "That guy didn't just buy a vehicle from us. He bought our reputation".'

As Rob started changing himself, others decided to join him on that life-long journey – people like Al Utesch. Al, who started out washing cars, years earlier, had thought about leaving. But there was something in this belief about getting outside yourself that sounded a lot like what his parents had taught him and what he was teaching his own children.

Then the Service Manager resigned and Rob felt that Al was the best candidate for the job, although not everyone else did – Al included. 'After 29 years in Parts, I was in the comfort zone,' he went on to say. 'I was scared to death, I spent the first two months staying awake at night.'

Rob says Al jumped in with both feet. 'He never even checked to see if the water was hot or cold. He never even asked about the pay.' In Al's opinion, the department's commitment to customer service was a joke. 'We talked about the issues and how to fix them. Some guys had been beaten up so much in the past they wanted to quit, but decided to give the new way a chance.' But other employees wanted no part of it. 'Some were key players, but they didn't want to go in the direction we were going,' recalls Rob. 'They were choosing not to be here. Knowing they'd produce a profit, I, as owner, looked at Al and said, "Will we let them go?" Al looked at our philosophy, mission and value cards and said, "Yes, let's move on".'

To replace those who had left, Al employed several people who had never been service advisors before. He took on people with energy, positive people, customer-orientated people, and then trained them with the necessary skills. Al also designed the service area. 'We used to open the doors at 6.45am. There were two lanes and customers were bumping into each other. It was like herding cattle.' Al changed it to a single lane, with reservations every 15 minutes. 'The goal was to give more personalised, quality time with the customer so the advisor could accurately report what the problem was.'

In a few months, the service department's customer satisfaction scores soared in the top 10% in the group. Profits and market share rose significantly. Employee satisfaction made the largest jump that Rob had ever seen. 'Before, we fixed cars,' Al said, 'But now I realise that we're looking after people.'

'There are days when I'm down and I don't believe it,' says Rob. 'Now Al comes and pumps me up, and I remember, Oh yeah! What we do *does* matter!'

Sharpen the saw – principles of balanced self-renewal

Bruce Barton wrote the following thoughts about the importance of everything we think and do.

> Sometimes when I consider what tremendous consequences come from little things ... So now I am tempted to think there are no little things.

In Stephen Covey's book *The Seven Habits of Highly Effective People*, he tells of someone working feverishly to saw down a tree. 'What are you doing?' you ask. 'Can't you see?' comes the reply, 'I'm sawing down this tree.'

'You look exhausted!' you exclaim. 'How long have you been at it?'

'Over five hours,' he replies, 'and I'm very tired, this is hard work.'

'Well, why don't you take a break for a few minutes and sharpen the saw?' you inquire. 'I'm sure it would go a lot faster.'

'I don't have time to sharpen the saw,' the man says emphatically, 'I'm too busy sawing.'

Can you relate to this man's situation? Many of us are so busy doing what we are doing that we are missing the opportunity of preserving and enhancing the greatest asset we have – ourselves.

We need to renew four dimensions of our natures – physical, spiritual, mental and social/emotional.

The physical dimension

This involves caring effectively for our physical body, eating the right foods, getting sufficient rest and relaxation, and exercising on a regular basis. Exercise is one of those high-leverage activities that lots of people don't do consistently because it doesn't appear to be urgent. If we don't exercise, sooner or later we will find ourselves dealing with health problems and crises originating as a natural result of our neglect. Most people think they don't have enough time to exercise. What a distorted paradigm! We don't have time not to. We're talking about three to six hours a week, or a minimum of thirty minutes a day, every other day. You don't need any special equipment to do it. If you want to go to the gym or a spa to use the equipment or enjoy some skill sports such as tennis or golf, that's an added opportunity.

The spiritual dimension

This is the core, your centre, your commitment to your value system. It's a very private area of your life and a supremely important one. It draws upon the sources that inspire and uplift you and tie you to the timeless truths of all humanity. By reading and/or by meditation you can feel renewed, strengthened, centred and recommitted to serve and deliver to everyone around you. Immersion in great literature or music can provide a similar renewal of the spirit for some. There are others who find it in their way to communicate with nature. When you are able to leave the noise of the city behind, and give yourself up to the harmony and rhythm of nature, you can return renewed and better able to cope with life in the sometimes hectic modern world.

The mental dimension

Most of our mental development and study discipline comes through formal education. But many of us, as we leave the external discipline of school, don't do any serious reading, don't explore new subjects in any real depth and don't always think analytically, and too many of us spend too much time watching TV. Like the body, television is a good servant but a poor master. Education – continuing education, honing and expanding the mind – provides vital mental renewal. Sometimes that involves the external discipline of systemised study programmes. Many proactive people can figure out many ways to educate themselves. In his book, Stephen Covey quotes Philip Brooks on this subject: 'Some day, in the years to come, you will be wrestling with the great temptation, or trembling under the great sorrow of your life. But the real struggle is here, now ... Now it is decided whether, in the day of your supreme sorrow or temptation, you shall miserably fail or gloriously conquer. Character cannot be made except by a steady, long continued process.'

The social / emotional dimension

This dimension is tied together because our emotional life is very much tied together with our relationships with others. We can renew our social and emotional dimension during our everyday transactions with people with whom we come into contact. Suppose that you are a key person in my life. You might be my boss, someone who works for me, a co-worker, my child, etc. – anyone with whom I want to interact. Suppose we have to communicate together, to discuss an issue, to accomplish a purpose or solve a problem. But we see things differently. I need to say to you, 'I can see that we're approaching this situation differently. Why don't we agree to communicate until we find a solution we both feel good about. Would you be willing to do that?' Most people would agree. I need to then say, 'let me listen to you first'. Once I listen intently and am able to explain your point of view as well as you can, then I can focus on communicating my point of view to you, so that you can understand as well.

Peace of mind comes when your life is in harmony with true principles and values and in no other way.

Develop a beginner's mind

In Nigel Barlow's book *Batteries Included*, he writes a chapter on developing a beginner's mind. He starts the subject with a quotation:

In the beginner's mind there are many possibilities, in the expert's there are few.' (Suzuki-roshi (1905–71), Japanese Zen Priest)

My interpretation of this is that we *all* forget to take that fresh look at situations at work and at home. We can't see the woods for the trees. We don't take time to review the way we do things or see things. We need to keep asking ourselves, 'What business are we in?' The answer determines where you focus your resources, time and energy, and the end result that the customer experiences. Using a beginner's mind can help you to review and then reframe what you're really offering the customer. What can move our perception beyond the influence of past experience? What can you see in the image below?

WRITING

WALL

At first, many people see a jumble of letters. Some see two words one on top of another, while others bring their eyes back from the page and eventually see the 'writing on the wall'. Several points come from this exercise. If people don't see it then you have to give them some clues to help them. To look at your business through the customer's eyes is as difficult as switching this image inside out. It is difficult to switch our thinking and walk in our 'customers shoes' as it means a complete switch of perception. Another problem or challenge is that once we see one solution, we stop looking for others. This demonstrates the problem of experience – it can become an inhibitor to change and innovation. A well-known phrase which illustrates this point comes from the manager who said, 'One month in this job and you go blind!' What he or she meant was that after the initial learning period of a job, *we* stop asking curious questions and challenging assumptions about how things are done, and worst of all, we often lose the ability to think for ourselves. The word amateur comes from the Latin *amare*, meaning to love. To have the attitude of an amateur means greater enjoyment in what you do.

How to be a top dog – love your job

Many successful companies say that to deliver top customer service you have to employ the right people, i.e. people who love what they do, and have lots of enthusiasm. The secret of superb service is to know that service is not a matter of servility and servitude but that of noble profession. However, the 'downstairs' psychology of many people providing service still persists, and many service providers like to demonstrate to customers in various subtle ways that they are just as good as their customers, and they want you to be sure of that. They don't enjoy their job, and want to share this information with their customers. People who love what they do are far less likely to suffer from stress. Surveys reflect that people who hate their job are far more likely to suffer from mental ill-health. But if your job appears to be lousy, what can you do? Here are three suggestions.

Find an enthusiast

You may feel that parts of your job are less enjoyable than others. This will be true for every profession. Let other people help you to gain some enthusiasm for these more mundane duties. We all know somebody who is able to maintain a positive approach to everything; let their upbeat optimism rub off on you. This can be a co-manager, co-worker, family member, friend or mentor. An injection of enthusiasm goes a long way!

Act 'as if'

When I first started as a trainer, a trainer friend said to me to just act 'as if' I was a great trainer and that I would be amazed by how this affected my approach and overall results. This advice definitely helped me, and although I still occasionally admit my incompetence with certain topics, overall the advice gave me a tremendous boost to my self-confidence and has helped me greatly to communicate what I did know.

Have fun

Many businesses have become very dull, serious, fear-driven places. It is not surprising how this affects the staff and in turn the customers. When people love what they do, it can't be anything but fun. South West Airlines suggest the following guidelines for their staff:

- Think funny and adopt a playful attitude; be the first to laugh.
- Laugh with, not at; laugh at yourself; take work seriously, but not yourself.

Building self-confidence and self-esteem

Some effects of low self-confidence can make people's lives unbearable.

Thinking. Some people programme negativity by what they think: 'I can't', 'That's too difficult', 'I don't know how', 'I just can't decide what to do', etc.

Feelings. People can feel apprehension; anticipatory anxiety; worry, especially about forthcoming difficulties;

frustration and anger with themselves; fear of the unknown or new situations; resentment – it seems so easy for others; discouragement and feeling demoralised.

Behaviour. This manifests itself by people taking a passive and less active role, and staying in the background. It can sometimes be difficult to make suggestions and put yourself forward, often taking a back seat, hesitating and repeatedly needing reassurance.

Bodily signs of low confidence. This is seen through poor posture, tending to stoop, not looking people in the eye, fumbling or fidgeting, feeling tense and nervous, being sluggish and lethargic.

Strategies for building confidence

1. Practice

The first time you tried to drive, you may have stalled the car, but by the time you passed your test, stalling the car was a thing of the past. Make building your confidence a habit – practising all the strategies below whenever you can. The more you practise, the more it becomes a habit and a skill, and the more secure your inner confidence will be.

2. Behave 'as if'

Ask yourself at a less than confident moment, 'How would I behave if I really felt confident?' 'How would x handle this?' (where x is a confident person who you know). Adopting the behaviour of confidence – posture, actions and thoughts – starts you on the upward spiral of increasing self-confidence.

3. Take a zig-zag path

It is important to be flexible with your approach and to pay attention to the techniques that work for you. Watch out for clues from others. Flexibility and confidence go hand in hand. Rigidity, even if it feels safer, gets in the way as no two situations are exactly the same.

Don't worry if you need to take a zig-zag path to your goal. People lacking self-confidence often feel that they have to take a careful and well-planned route to avoid pitfalls. These pitfalls are often imaginary, and the fear of taking a wrong step can become inhibiting and counter-productive.

4. Make the most of your mistakes, then ignore them

What matters is not doing something wrong, nor doing something badly, but whether you recognise the mistake and use it to try to set yourself on a better path next time. Samuel Beckett said, 'No matter. Try again. Fail again. Fail better.' Errors are for learning. Only those who have ceased to develop never take a wrong step. Mistakes are a source of information. The key message is to learn from the mistake and then ignore it.

5. Limit self-blame

Apply the 'water-under-the-bridge' rule, and operate a statute of limitations. Kicking yourself for past inadequacies, confusions or failures gives fuel to your internal wavering voice – cut off its supply of oxygen and use encouraging messages to yourself instead. Imagine that you have a champion whose job it is to bring the best out of you. What encouraging things would this person be saying to you? Remind yourself of these messages; you are as capable as anyone!

6. Be kind to yourself

Problems with self-confidence are often rooted in a bad habit of punishing ourselves and failing to seek out rewards and pleasures. If the habit of self-punishment is reversed, and you learn to treat yourself correctly, your self-confidence will be able to grow.

Improve your memory

There are no sure-fire strategies to developing a super memory, but some of the suggestions below have produced startling results.

Practise a skill – a little and often

This has been tested with typing skills, and on average it was found that those who practised four hours a day took 80 hours to reach a competent standard, whereas those who practised one hour a day took just 55 hours.

Mnemonics

'Richard of York gave battle in vain' is a mnemonic device which many of us learned as children to remember the colours of the rainbow (red, orange, yellow, green, blue, indigo, violet). If something you have to remember seems nonsense to you, or comes in a string of disconnected bits, like a list of facts, names or numbers, then the best thing to do is try and make sense of it in any way you can. Sing it, make up a rhyme, transform the words into a visual image, tell yourself a story and it will almost always become more memorable.

Important information is easier to remember

Things that stand out for some reason (your first day at school, something embarrassing, first kiss, etc.) will stick in your memory. Unimportant things can become more memorable, by making them more *vivid* or by giving them a personal meaning. A bright yellow folder will be harder to leave behind than a black one, or writing your name on it will make it more likely to draw your attention to it, rather than writing a bland heading such as 'notes' or 'memos'.

It is important to forget things

You have sometimes to prioritise your thinking, so you need to tell yourself what to forget. You will remember best those things that you pay attention to, but if everything grabs your attention, your memory will be overloaded. You can reduce the load by concentrating on the important tasks and issues.

You need time for digestion

Sometimes you can feel confused or muddled. However, after a pause or a rest you may be able to make more sense of particular information and remember it better. This is evident sometimes when learning a mind and body skill, e.g. a computer software programme or typing skills. If you push yourself too far in one go, you start to make mistakes and your performance will deteriorate. If you rest, you will find that your performance improves. Your mind continues learning after you have stopped practising.

Four ideas to try

1. The more you use the information, the more memorable it becomes.

2. Give your mind space to work.

3. It is easier to recognise things than to recall them.

4. Association works wonders.

Do you enjoy what you do?

Most people who work say they need the money. Few are fortunate enough to be able to ignore paid employment for long. But in surveys, people often say they would keep working even if they did not need the money. Some lottery winners are examples of this and prove this point.

Simon Fullerton-Ballantyne won £1.89 million in the lottery. He quit work but later returned to buy the company. He says, 'It's not the money that makes me come to work. You have to have something to get up for in the morning otherwise you might as well not exist.'

Roger Robar won £5.8 million and bought a restaurant he once worked in. He cooks there three nights a week and says, 'Cooking is in my blood. If I can't cook, I'm miserable ... Why stop doing something that makes me happy?'

Economists have a label for this sort of behaviour. They attribute it to the rise of 'post-scarcity' society. In advanced economies, the time when people were working to provide themselves with the things they need has long gone. Yet people do work, and work hard. If the purpose of that work was merely the acquisition of desirable consumer items – stuff we want but don't need – then lottery winners would quit at once. What is it that drives rich people to stay in their often low-paid, low-skill jobs?

Robert Wuthrow, who teaches cultural sociology at the University of California, argues that in a post-scarcity society, 'the values associated with work shift increasingly toward emotional and intellectual gratification, collegiality, and service'. He quotes from a speech given to a group of students by the chairman of a large company. 'Since work we must, like breathing in and breathing out, let me share the greatest secret in the world with you. I tell you that good, first-rate work is glory.' In the course of his speech the chairman described what he meant:

- 'good work separates humankind from the beasts;
- good human work puts us all together;
- good work builds;
- good work adds to the sum of humanity;
- good work pays;
- good work makes us matter;
- good work is fun.'

Robert Wuthnow uses this speech as a prime example of the new formulation of work. 'In place of the work-for-money argument that seems of so little use, I want to suggest an alternative perspective: that people work in order to give a legitimate account of themselves.' Accounts are sociology-speak for stories – for the scripts we write in our lives. As Wuthnow puts it, accounts are a 'vital element of the process by which we ascribe meaning to our behaviour'.

In a world in which other forms of account, such as where you are born, which God you worship or your family situation (place, faith and blood), have declined in importance, work has acquired new salience. Our work is the principal character in the story of ourselves.

4

Managing stress

Ten ways to combat stress

1. *Change your viewpoint.* Refuse to let others stress you. View rudeness and sarcasm as personality defects, which are the problems of others rather than a reflection of your own abilities. Never bear grudges. John Kennedy once said, 'Forgive your enemies, just never forget their names.' Say something nice to another person at least once a day. Paying compliments makes two people feel good. Adopt the philosophy that 'nothing in life matters too much, and most things do not matter at all.'

2. *Put your problems into perspective.* Everybody has problems (challenges) or lives with problems, but few of these problems are truly catastrophic. Break big problems into smaller ones and solve them one at a time. Be optimistic. Regard mistakes and setbacks as opportunities to learn. Always try and discover something good in whatever happens to you, no matter how bad it appears to be initially.

3. *Laugh at life.* Studies show nursery-age children laugh an average of 450 times a day, adults only 15 times a day. Become childlike in your sense of fun and ability to see the ridiculous side of human experience.

4. *Stop worrying and start working.* 'Worry' comes from the Anglo-Saxon word meaning to *strangle* or *choke*, and it prevents you from thinking or acting effectively. One of the worst times for worrying is in the early hours of the morning, when things can seem at their bleakest. This is the time when our metabolism runs slowly, body temperature is at its lowest and blood glucose level is low. This physical slowing down, produced by our body-clock, contributes significantly to the sense of despair and hopelessness that many experience.

   – Instead of tossing and turning, distract yourself by listening to soothing music, read an amusing book or try out a relaxation exercise (see point 7).

   – Stop fretting and start working to change the situation that you find intolerable.

   – Ralph Waldo Emerson once said, 'Do the thing you fear most, and the death of fear is certain.'

5. *Stop talking yourself down.* Self-deprecating comments and gloomy inner dialogues undermine confidence and create needless stress.

   – Say positive confidence-boosting phrases to yourself, e.g. 'Every day, in every way, I'm getting better and better!' It makes good sense.

   – When you do well congratulate yourself. If you fail to achieve a goal then tell yourself: 'I didn't succeed this time, but I know what I did wrong. Next time I'll get it right.'

6. *Slow your life down.* Even if you live life in the fast lane, your mind and body needs will change in pace. In the evenings, at weekends, on short breaks or longer holidays you must discipline yourself to slow down.

- Take up a hobby that cannot be rushed, e.g. cooking, model making, gardening, pottery.
- Take a stroll in the country or in your local park, pausing deliberately every now and again to look at the views.
- Read a non-work-related book.
- Study yoga and meditation, i.e. sit down alone in a room without distractions for ten minutes, concentrate on a single thought and breath deeply.

7. *Sooth away your stress.* Massage is simple; here are simple guidelines:

- using your fingertips, gently massage around the eyes in a circular motion;
- repeat three more times;
- apply fingertip pressure to both sides of your temple, starting at the nose, make a series of circular movements across your brow, across the temple and then around the cheekbone;
- complete by rubbing your hands together then place them lightly over your eyes and forehead. Feel the warmth easing away any lingering tension.

8. *Unwind at the end of the day.* Sit down at the end of the day, half close your eyes and focus on a spot on the ground a few feet in front of you. Breathe slowly and deeply, concentrating on the spot. Try and focus for 60 seconds. After 60 seconds, get up and return to your normal routine, carrying feelings of controlled mental relaxation.

9. *Reduce physical stress through relaxation.* Tense your hands, arms, eyes, legs, neck, etc., for ten seconds and relax. Feel the tension disappear.

10. *Exercise away your stress*. Moderate but regular exercise, which raises your resting heart rate, can work wonders in reducing stress. Walk, jog, swim, cycle; what you do doesn't really matter as long as you do it for at least 20 minutes at a time.

Relax and take the stress test

Death is nature's way of telling you to slow down. (Anon.)

Do you have 'hurry sickness'?

People who feel constantly tired, irritable, anxious, demoralised and depressed are showing definite signs of 'hurry sickness.' When you can't concentrate, it is difficult to make decisions, and this can lead to a series of errors. This can have a knock-on effect in the workplace, as deadlines will be missed, and a backlog of uncompleted tasks can make the position even worse. Sleepless nights can be a result because of the worry caused.

Symptoms of 'hurry sickness' include:

- not having enough time each day to meet the demands made on you;

- feeling angry and frustrated by delays, however unavoidable they may be;

- attempting to do everything at the double (immediately);

- an inability to relax even on holiday;

- a lack of patience when dealing with people less fast paced than yourself;

- leaving things to the last minute;
- needing a 'deadline high' to motivate yourself.

Hurry sickness is also associated with serious health problems, including high blood pressure, ulcers, strokes and heart disease. So what can be done to break free from this vicious and potentially fatal cycle?

Today most people regard stress as a form of torture. The truth is that stress can be either your friend or your foe. When used correctly, stress releases hidden reserves of creative energy, enabling you to enjoy a healthier, happier and more fulfilling life.

60-second stress test

Are you a victim of hurry sickness? Take this 60-second test and find out.

Without looking at your watch, or secretly counting seconds, estimate the passing of one minute. When you think time is up, check to see how much time has actually elapsed. What your result reveals:

- *Less than 55 seconds* – You are a victim of hurry sickness: you need to study the notes on how to relax and reduce needless stress by managing your time more effectively.

- *Between 55 and 65 seconds* – You may feel that there are still too few hours in the day to accomplish all you need to achieve. Studying the notes on relaxation and reading reducing stress techniques will also be useful to you.

- *More than 65 seconds* – You have a relaxed attitude to the passing of time, and dislike having to race against the clock. Enjoy yourself!

Peak performance level

Yuri Hanin, a Russian sports psychologist, suggested some time ago that athletic success was associated with an optimal level of mental and physical alertness. Today, it is accepted that this is true in all spheres of life. We all have a level of alertness at which mind and body function best. This is called our peak performance stress level (PPSL).

- When there is *too little stress* we feel bored, apathetic and lacking in motivation. In this state of mind, time seems to slow to a snail's pace.

- *Too much stress* produces anxiety, confusion and a sapping of self-confidence. In this mental state, time often rushes past, making it hard to complete tasks, solve problems or make decisions.

- At our *peak of alertness* (PPSL) we feel energetic, enthusiastic, confident and, above all, in control of events.

In the future, when faced with a task that offers too little stimulating stress, consider ways of increasing your level of alertness:

- Break a major task into smaller ones that you can complete more quickly and easily.

- Undertake the task during your biological prime time, when you will be able to focus all your energy on the challenge.

- Delegate those aspects of the job which you consider especially less stimulating.

See if you can do the same task to a higher level, so as to introduce a greater sense of challenge. But this should only be done when the greater demands allow you to achieve your goals more effectively.

Relaxation – the gift of life

Relaxation is the gift of achieving physical and mental ease in your body. It is knowing that you belong and where you belong. Without a minimum amount of true relaxation, we undertake any task from a disadvantaged basis. Humans simply were not made to stay in a state of stress all the time.

When the hormones that trigger the fight or flight response were pumping through the bodies of our prehistoric ancestors, they were almost always facing a physical stressor; they either killed the wild and woolly mammoth or were killed by it. For us today, most stress is not physical but psychological or spiritual. If you get an unfair evaluation at work because of a petty jealousy of your boss, what can you do?: fight (which means confronting your boss or other parties, even though you know that you will lose) or flight (which means quitting your job and starting over)? Generally we can do neither. Both responses are unsatisfactory.

But our bodies are made to do one or the other and hormones are pumping through our veins for that purpose. The negative stress energy has to go somewhere and do something. It does not go away on its own. Most often, what it does is attack its host – you. You get sick, irritable, have backaches, flu, colds, lose or gain weight; whatever form your stress takes. However, you *can* do something about it.

Regain control

People today have never experienced true relaxation and therefore all their projects begin with a handicap. Perhaps they lived with so much tension and stress in their childhood that they are unaware of what they are carrying and it feels normal to them. That's a serious problem. Learning how to relax is crucial to our physical and emotional well-being.

Once you have experienced stress in your life, you need to do something with that negative stress energy in order to balance the time of stress with an opposite time of being relaxed. You just can't return to normal without relaxation time and expect a real recovery from the stress. Remember, the negative stress energy does not go away by itself: it accumulates and, if not balanced by a time of relaxation, continues to do you harm. Understanding this is the key to true relaxation.

Keeping control

Your life can bob along with little or no stress, then a stress event occurs, e.g. someone recklessly cuts out in front of you in traffic, nearly causing an accident and scaring you enough to make your heart pound and your muscles tighten from a rush of adrenaline. The stress event moves you up through the alarm stage and above into stress territory. It would be common for one to feel and be affected by this event for days after. There is a resistance stage during which you actually spend time coping with the stress. This can last from a few days to several months.

If you merely return to your normal lifestyle, you have not fully recovered from the stress. You still carry the effects of the stress though you may not be aware of them; they accumulate with others that are already there. For real recovery, you must go below the stress threshold and fully relax for a time, and then return back to normal living. Only then will you have truly recovered. For every occasion that you go above your stress threshold, you must balance it by going below it. The times don't have to be equal, but you do need time in both territories for real recovery.

Stopping

Stopping is spending time below the stress threshold, and relaxation can bring real relief for the first time in people's lives. This is especially true of those who have lived with long-term stressors such as chronic illness (of self and others), abusive relationships, unfair work situations, unavoidable meanness, and moments of crisis where anxiety is normal. It also applies to many people who have slipped into workaholism.

What does time below the stress threshold look like? It will be different for everyone and even different at various times of your life. It may involve walking, swimming, loafing at your ease, watching trees or reading poetry? The essential characteristic of time below the threshold is recovery of balance.

Still-points are the good friends of relaxation. Breathing and remembering are natural relaxants: they cause the body's automatic nervous system to relax and recover. To increase the relaxation factor, add a few stretches, notice where you are holding tension in your body, and then breathe relaxing energy into it.

Enjoying exercise

Have you ever said, 'I must start doing some more regular exercise?' More and more people are saying it, but what about doing something about it? There are also people who say (and you could be one of them), 'But I just haven't the time to do any exercise.' Well there are many ways that you can embrace some physical activity that fits into your schedule – whether or not you get to the gym or even change into exercise gear. Below are a few possibilities.

No-time exercises

Here are a few ways that you can exercise without having necessarily to plan large chunks of time:

- walk to work or run for the train;
- take the dog for a walk;
- walk with a pushchair;
- take the stairs between floors in the building where you work;
- play sports with your kids in the park or garden;
- do some gardening chores with your own hands or hand tools rather than electric machine tools – cutting the grass, trimming hedges, pulling weeds, raking up leaves.

Balance your exercise

Unless you are an elite athlete, the trick to exercises is to match them and balance one against another, each providing an advantage that your other activities do not. It's all a matter of balance. Here are three mixing principles to help you guide you in your choice:

- *Match skill with repetition.* There are certain forms of exercise, such as running and swimming, that involve repetitive, familiar movements in which the mind is free to wander. Mix these with other sports in which high levels of skill are required, so that the body and mind are taken in entirely different directions. High-skill activities include skiing, football, mountain-biking, racquet sports and golf.

- *Combine hard and soft high-impact sports.* Running and tennis can jar the joints. Mix in some sports that are less abusive on the body. Good examples are cycling, swimming and rowing.

- *Combine upper and lower body exercise.* Both running and cycling target lower body muscle groups, and leave the upper body largely unimproved. Aim for the whole-body workout. Possible combinations are listed below. Combine any sport in the left-hand column with any sport in the right-hand column:

walking	swimming
running	rowing
biking	canoeing
skiing	tennis

Three ways to make training easier

1. *Write it down.* Keep track of your progress in a training log. This not only records how well you're sticking to your plan, it also provides a sense of accomplishment. Don't just write down times and distances – note things like your frame of mind or how tired you felt. These can help you sense what works for you and what doesn't, so you can fine-tune your programme.

2. *Enlist friends.* Training alone can become dull and discouraging. Training with one or more friends or colleagues can provide support, create camaraderie and inspiration, as well as introduce competition. It also helps motivate you because you are less likely to miss a workout if your friends are counting on you to be there.

3. *Keep it convenient.* Make sure that the bulk of your training can take place somewhere that's easy to get to, close to your home or workplace. The more you have to

travel or if you burden yourself with logistical complications, the harder it will be.

Ways to stay motivated

You need to have a strategy to prevent you from becoming fed up and losing interest.

- *Set goals*. It's good to have an outcome in mind. For example, 'I will run 3 miles twice this week', is much better than 'I will take up running.' When your goals become stale, just set new ones.

- *Don't compare*. There will always be some people who are fitter and stronger than you. Ignore them, as the only focus you really need is on your own immediate capabilities (and limitations) and how they improve.

- *Lighten up*. If you slacken off sometimes, that's alright. Fitness losses, like gains, occur slowly. Maybe you need a break. That's not a failure, and it's not a reason to quit.

- *Have fun*. Working out should be a pleasure, not a chore. Cruising down a hill on a bike or making love is work but not drudgery. Neither are 20 minutes on a stationary bike or weight repetitions if you know they will make these more exciting activities better later.

A fast train on a fast track

Do you ever feel that life is moving at a frantic pace and that you are moving along in a fast train? Slowing down doesn't necessarily work as everything around us is going so fast. We get revved-up even if we don't want to be. Stephan Rechtschaffen, MD (a pioneer of the wellness movement and Holistic Studies and is based at the Omega campus near New York), has written in his book *Timeshifting* about 'entrainment', which he describes as an unconscious process that governs how various rhythms fall into sync with one another. For example, if you put two out-of-sync pendulum clocks next to each other, in a short time, they would be exactly in sync. The same principle works with atomic particles, the tides and humans. Human beings pick up one another's rhythms and the accumulated rhythms of the world around us. If most of the rhythms around us are fast, so are ours, automatically. That's entrainment. The word can also mean 'getting on a train.'

We have all boarded the train, the fast train on the fast track, and the process of entrainment is not under our conscious control. That's why trying to slow down doesn't slow us down. It's not because we're weak willed or quitters, it's because we're on a fast train where we are the passengers and not the engineers.

We are all riding on a very fast train that is travelling down a predetermined track, gathering speed as it goes, and we have been on it for a long time. We can't get to the engineer because the engineer is protected by loyal guards. Perhaps there is no engineer and the train is run by a computer. Many of us want to slow down, some want to get off the train. Others are so used to the speed that they don't notice it. A few love the speed and want to increase it. The few who love the speed are the only ones who get their way. Most of us stare blankly out the window barely seeing the world flying by.

Fortunately, there is something we can do about it. Stopping can get us off the train, can separate us from the speeded-up rhythms of those around us, and can bring us into rhythms of our own choosing, which may include some time on the fast train.

Stopping can roll us into the sidings for refreshment and cool off so we can make sure that, when we take off again, we're on the right track, going in the right direction and have an intimate working relationship with the engineer.

Entrainment helps us explain the amazingly short attention span of most of us nowadays. We get our information in soundbites: many brief, skeletal bones of facts. We just don't have the time to read in depth or to linger over the newspaper. It seems also to have something to say about our fad-driven society. As soon as one idea, trend, fashion or person becomes popular, it is quickly dropped for whatever next demands our attention. Whether it is valuable or vulgar seems to make no difference; it's just the next view out of the window of the fast train. We can find ourselves, unwittingly, screaming through the night on the fast train and trying to figure out, 'How did I get here?'

Stopping can bring about an answer and a solution.

Three ways of stopping

> Finally it has penetrated my thick skull. This life, this moment, is no dress rehearsal. This is it! (F. Knebel)

Stopping has three levels. They are based on length of time: 'still-points', 'stopovers' and 'grinding halts'. All are effective, but each one is meant for different moments of life.

A still-point is stopping quickly and doing nothing for just a moment. It is brief and meant to be used anytime, all the time (every day) and many times a day. Still-points are essentially very short: a few seconds or a few minutes. They are designed to take advantage of unfilled moments of life: waiting for the kettle to boil, brushing your teeth or sitting at red traffic lights. They are also good for handling moments of stress, e.g. walking into an interview, during a moment of anger, or when you know that you are going to be late for an appointment.

Less frequent are stopovers, which are those times that are longer than a still-point, an hour to several days. These are wonderful times of stopping, when you really have a feeling that you have been away and have had a mini-break for the soul. The most common expression of the stopover is the afternoon, day or weekend away, whether you go anywhere or not.

Grinding halts will probably happen only a couple of times in most people's lives. They are periods from a week to a month – or more. They need to be planned, require a large and deeper commitment of time and energy, and typically happen at times of life transitions.

Each of the three levels of stopping is effective. The more frequent the repetitions or the longer the time, the more lasting the effect. Think of the three levels as going down (each one deeper and more effective) and plumbing the deeper recesses of your being, allowing you creatively and joyfully to do nothing and to become more fully awake and re-collected. These experiences will help you to make accurate decisions and to maintain your true life-direction.

Still-points, stopovers and grinding halts should be used to help you keep one thing clearly in your mind: all you have is 'now', 'then' is gone and 'when' is not yet and may never be. As the quote at the beginning of this topic reminds us, this is not a dress rehearsal for life, which will happen sometime later when you are more prepared. You are not waiting for anything to begin; you are in the middle of it.

Take care of yourself now; seize the day!

The wonders of sleep

Most people spend about eight hours out of 24, or one-third of their entire life, asleep. This also applies to the animal and vegetable worlds.

People get tired during the day, and they go to sleep to rest the body, and a reparative process takes place while you sleep. Nothing rests in sleep. Your heart, lungs and all your vital organs remain functioning. Food is digested, skin secretes perspiration, and your nails and hair continue to grow. Your subconscious mind never rests or sleeps. It is always active, controlling all your vital forces. The healing process takes place more rapidly while you are asleep as there is no interference from your conscious mind. Remarkable answers are given to you while you are asleep.

Sleep relaxes you and restores your spirit

Dr John Bigelow, an authority on sleep, found in his studies that the results strengthened his convictions that the supposed exemption from normal activities was not the final purpose of sleep, but rather to help develop spiritual well-being. Your conscious mind gets involved with annoyances, worries and issues every day, and it is necessary to withdraw periodically from evidence from your senses and the objective world, and commune silently with the inner wisdom of your subconscious mind. By claiming guidance, strength and greater intelligence in all phases of your life, you will be enabled to overcome all difficulties and solve daily problems. This regular break from sense evidence and the noise and confusion of everyday living is also a form of sleep, i.e. you become asleep to the world of senses and alive to the wisdom of your subconscious mind.

Sleep in peace and wake refreshed

To anyone who suffers from insomnia, you will find the following technique very effective. Repeat it slowly, quietly and consistently prior to sleep: 'My toes are relaxed, my ankles are relaxed, my abdominal muscles are relaxed, my hands and arms are relaxed, my neck is relaxed, my eyes are relaxed, my whole mind and body are relaxed. I am at peace, poised and calm. I freely forgive everyone, I sincerely wish them harmony and goodwill. I look forward to a good night's sleep and I will awake in good humour, relaxed and refreshed.' Try it out, it really works!

Key benefits of sleep

- If you are afraid that you will sleep in, suggest to your subconscious the time you want to get up, and it will waken you. It needs no clock. Do the same with all problems; there is nothing too hard for your subconscious.

- Your subconscious never sleeps. It is always working, it controls all your vital functions. Forgive yourself and everyone else before you go to sleep, and healing will take place more rapidly.

- Guidance is given while you sleep, sometimes in a dream. The healing currents are also released, and in the morning you will feel refreshed and rejuvenated.

- When troubled by worries, focus your thinking to the wisdom and intelligence that is lodged in your subconscious mind, which is ready to respond to you. This will give you peace, strength and confidence.

- Sleep is essential for peace of mind and health of body. Lack of sleep can cause irritation, depression and mental disorders. You need eight hours of sleep.

- You are spiritually recharged during sleep.

- Sleep-deprived people generally have poorer memories and lack proper co-ordination.

- Sleep helps you solve challenges. Before sleep, ask yourself the questions that trouble you, and take note of the thoughts that you wake up with.

- Trust your subconscious; it helps you as you sleep.

- Your future is in your mind now, based on your habitual thinking and beliefs. Expect the best, and invariably the best will come to you.

If you are working on a project, hobby or pastime, speak to your subconscious mind at night and claim that its wisdom and power is guiding and revealing to you the best solution to your worries or challenges. Focus on finding answers and you will not only access answers but you will begin to expect results as a norm.

Breathing is inspiring – try it, it really works

A friend of mine said to me recently, 'I'll never forget the moment I learned to breathe. No, it wasn't when the doctor slapped my bottom as a welcome to the world and I gulped my first intake of air. It was 50 years later when I was training to become an interactive guided image therapist. During one of the sessions, we were led through a breathing exercise. The woman leading the group spoke, slowly, calmly and clearly about the process of breathing and how many of us breathe shallowly. That teaching changed my life, because as I breathed deeply in and then completely exhaled, involving the entire internal mechanisms of the diaphragmatic breath, the experience was so new and overwhelming. As I continued to breathe consciously and fully, I began to shake, because the experience was so physically and emotionally revolutionary. I know it sounds odd, but in the days and weeks that followed, I became much more conscious of my breathing, practising frequently and learning the nuances of breathing.'

Conscious breathing means to breathe deeply and intentionally. To breathe deeply is to begin the breathe low in your belly and move it into your chest.

To learn how to do this, begin by placing your left hand over your heart and your right hand over your belly button. As you breathe in, your right hand should move out and away from your body as your lungs fill with air, and your left hand should remain still. The movement should make you look fatter than you are; your stomach should be protruding. Then, as you exhale, your right hand should move back towards your body, and your left hand should remain still. The taking in of air moves your stomach, not your chest, out.

Too often what happens is that we take a deep breath, the left hand on the chest moves out, meaning that the air is kept shallow and high in the chest and does not bring oxygen to the lungs in an efficient way.

To take this a step further, begin with your hands placed as above: left hand on your heart and right hand on your belly button. Breathe in and watch your right hand move out. But this time, continue to breathe in and when the right hand is out as far as is comfortable, bring the inhale up to your chest and allow the left hand to move out also.

Then, as you exhale, the reverse movement happens as your left hand moves close to the body first and the right hand follows. As you take these breaths in succession, you will see that there is an undulating motion as air moves from down to up and up to down: from the stomach to the chest and the chest to the stomach.

This is conscious breathing and it brings several profound benefits. It deepens your awareness of this particular moment and brings you directly into contact with the present. It internally massages the major internal organs, relaxing them, and creates a heightened awareness of yourself and, by its very nature, causes you to expand both spiritually and physically. *Spirit* and *breath* are the same root; *inspiration* means to breathe in. Breathing is inspiring.

Many people might think that breathing is an involuntary activity of the human body, and it seems silly to practise or improve it. But many of us breathe shallowly and at times, particularly during stress, we hold our breath so that we scarcely breathe at all. In order to experience the power of intentional breathing, begin by noticing how to breathe, when you hold your breath in and keep it tight (notice this especially when you are concentrating on something or trying to do detailed work) and how it feels when you take a deep, intentional breath.

There is a famous story from the Old Testament that applies here: Naaman was a powerful army general who became very ill. He consulted many wise physicians and healers, none of whom could restore his health. Word came to him from a servant girl that Elisha, a wise and powerful prophet in the neighbouring country, could cure him. So, in desperation, Naaman and his retinue travelled to Elisha in the distant country. When they found him, Naaman humbly made his request that the prophet use his powers to heal him.

Elisha simply told Naaman to bathe seven times in the River Jordan and he would be cured. The general was infuriated. 'We have rivers at home and I bathe in them every day, and what possible good will come of just bathing in a river! This is nonsense. We have wasted our time and effort.' Naaman was prepared to go. His servants, however, thinking that they had come such a long way convinced him that it would do no harm to try, and convinced the reluctant general to bathe seven times in the River Jordan. He did so and was cured.

Like Naaman, we tend to underestimate the power of something as ordinary as 'breathing' and we are tempted to think, 'I've been breathing since the day I was born, I don't need to learn to breathe at this point in my life.' Please don't think this way, just humour me; why not just give it a try. Just trust in the benefits of deep breathing on your physical and emotional state. It really works, if you work!

Learn how to relax

Do you ever lie awake at night feeling tired, tense and worried? Is it difficult to reach a peaceful state of mind? You can rely on both your mind and your body to do the job for you. There are four key steps to go through that can help you relax properly.

Step one: preparation

- Choose a method that attracts you, and stick to it.
- Schedule a time each day when you can practise, undisturbed, for 20–30 minutes.
- Find a comfortable place for your daily practice.

Learn to relax at your own pace; the more you rush, the harder it can become. Deep muscle relaxation uses the pendulum method – if you want the pendulum to swing in the opposite direction, you first have to pull it back. So practice involves tightening up muscle groups and then letting them go. The aim is to work systematically through the body, and it is usual to start with the hands, work up to the shoulders, then down your body towards the feet. It is best to settle down in a warm and comfortable place and wear loose clothing.

Tune into your breathing, and tell yourself to 'let go' as you breathe out. You can tell how you are doing by putting one hand on your chest and the other on your stomach and feeling them move.

Step two: practise

1. *Basic exercise.* Turn your attention to your hands. When you are ready, tighten up all the muscles in both hands. Clench your fists, and hold the tension while you count slowly up to three (pulling the pendulum back), then let the tension go. Feel the tension drain out of your fingers, and let them come naturally to rest. Each time you breathe out allow your hands to become heavier. Let the blood circulate freely right to your fingertips, as you feel more and more deeply relaxed. Give yourself as much time as you like to focus on your hands before you repeat the exercise with the next muscle group.

2. *Deep muscular relaxation.* Here is an order of muscle groups to try. Remember after tensing each group, let go slowly, feeling the tension drain away and the blood flowing freely. Don't forget to breathe.

- Hands: clench fists and let go.
- Arms: tighten biceps and lower arms together.
- Shoulders: raise your shoulders as if they could touch your ears.
- Feet: screw up your toes.
- Front of legs: point your foot away from you so that it is almost parallel with your leg.
- Back of legs: flex your feet upwards, stretching your heels down.
- Thighs: tighten them while pressing your knees down to the floor.
- Bottom: clench your buttocks together.
- Stomach: hold your stomach muscles in tightly.
- Lower back: press the small of your back into the floor.
- Chest: breathe in, hold your breath, and tighten all your chest muscles.
- Shoulders: breathe in, hold your breath and raise your shoulders as if they could touch your ears.
- Neck: (1) stretch your head up, as if your chin could touch the ceiling; (2) bend your head forward until your chin reaches your chest.
- Mouth and jaw: press your lips together and clench your teeth.
- Eyes: close them up tight.
- Forehead and scalp: raise your eyebrows as if they could disappear.
- Face: screw all the muscles together.

3. *Relaxing mentally as well as physically.* Make a list of places or situations that you find calming or relaxing, and

as you relax after doing your exercises, imagine that you really are in one of them. Do not worry if the images keep changing – imagery is rarely static. Don't let your problems take over, just imagine your place of calm and peace, e.g. woodland, the beach, sailing, hill-walking.

Step three: application

The reality of living on a day-to-day basis dictates that it is not possible to remain in a deeply relaxed state all the time. You have to learn how to recognise small degrees of tension early and how to let them go before they build up. This can be achieved by shortening the exercise, so that you can relax quickly, and by practising in increasingly difficult situations; for example, a quick-fix routine would be – tune into your breathing, take a deep breath in, hold it, and then tell yourself 'let go' as you breathe out. Repeat this several times, choosing an appropriate instruction to give yourself: 'Keep calm', 'Slow down', 'Let go.' Tense up and then relax muscle groups, hands, feet, stomach, etc.

Step four: develop a relaxed attitude

Relaxation is an attitude, a habit and a restorative as well as a skill. Make it part of your life:

- adopt a relaxed posture and stop rushing about;
- make a habit of doing things you find relaxing, e.g. reading, swimming, playing squash, doing nothing;
- seek out pleasures and treats, and give yourself short breaks;
- spread the risks, 'don't put all your eggs in one basket.'

Are you going stale in your job?

Many people say that one of the demons of the modern workplace is burnout – what happens when workers simply can't cope with the demands made upon them. Burnout equals exhaustion, breakdown, losing it.

Real burnout is terrible, the work equivalent of a heart attack. It usually happens only when someone ignores all the warning signs: feeling depressed, bitter, trapped, sleepless, etc. It doesn't happen to people who love their work, but does happen to people who feel forced into sticking at unsatisfactory jobs.

Philosopher Michel de Montaigne said that people who don't listen to their boredom threshold when reading a book are like those who ignore their pain threshold. The same is true of jobs. Ignoring the boredom threshold is like ignoring all those chest pains – and then wondering how on earth that burnout/heart attack could have happened.

There is, in any case, a much greater danger than burnout. People who stay in jobs that no longer stimulate or satisfy them are exposed to a much more widespread affliction, which is called 'rustout syndrome' according to Richard Leider, the author of *The Power of Purpose*. Leider describes a senior executive: 'He felt trapped in a kind of vocational quicksand. He was not challenged. He felt he could not leave, nor could he succeed. In short, he was rusting out.' Rustout happens to someone who is not challenged by meaningful tasks and is spared the positive stress surrounding such tasks.

Karl Marx identified a kind of rustout syndrome in his description of alienated labour, work in which the worker does not develop his physical and mental energy but mortifies his body and ruins his soul.

Some jobs 'mortify' from the beginning; the only mystery is why anybody stays in them or why society tolerates them. But even the best of jobs can lose their appeal after a while. For people who thirst to learn and stretch, the feeling of becoming good at their task quickly evaporates to be replaced by a sense of boredom as soon as they can do it. Leider says, 'the fact is that satisfaction always leads to dissatisfaction!'

A recent survey by the Chartered Institute of Personnel Directors confirmed that the longer people have been in their jobs, the less likely they will find them satisfying. Once we accept that work is part of our journey of self-exploration, a lifelong learning opportunity, we shouldn't find this either surprising or unsettling. Once the learning curve begins to level out, our interest drops too. If we stay put, we can become rustout risks.

The lesson to this: if you can do it, stop doing it and go and do something more interesting instead.

People who are in jobs they can 'do with their eyes closed' have almost certainly closed their eyes.

Work can be a happy pill!

Despite all the improvements relating to work over recent years – the increased room for growth and learning, the opportunities for self-development, the chance to work in a great team of people, the chance to write our own work script – there is still the ingrained attitude that happiness lies outside work. Most people are waiting for the weekend. Friday has a magical status in the anti-work world. Many celebrate Fridays with happy hours while others say, 'It's Friday, it's five o'clock, it's Crackerjack.'

For many, work is a time of woe, while holidays are a happy time. The notion that we are happier when we are not working is so deeply embedded that it is difficult to challenge. But the plain fact is: many people are happier at work! You may not think this, but it is true.

Mihaly Csikszentmihalyi in his book *Flow – The Psychology of Optimal Experience* writes that work is the real source of happiness. Csikszentmihalyi examines the true nature of happiness. He argues persuasively that happiness involves a lack of self-consciousness, an absorption. This is often lost when you ask yourself if you are happy and you cease to be so. Csikszentmihalyi talks about a happy state when people are so involved in the activity that nothing else seems to matter. He calls this state 'flow.'

Small children are often in 'flow' or 'in the moment', tongues pressed against lips as they colour or do dot-to-dot. Some of us still do it. Athletes describe the feeling as being 'in the zone'. Flow occurs when we are engaged and absorbed, when our minds are wrapped up in the project at hand. It is not quite the same feeling as pleasure, which often comes later.

When Csikszentmihalyi asked people to register times when they felt in flow, he found to his surprise that work was a clear winner. Half the time people were at work they were in 'flow', compared with 18% in their leisure time. Manager-level workers were in flow more often than blue-collar workers (64% versus 47%), but both experienced flow at work much more often than at home.

Csikszentmihalyi also asked people to record when they would 'rather be doing something else' during a particular period of time, and found that it was more likely when they were at work. He calls this the 'work paradox.'

In other words, motivation was low at work even when it provided flow, and it was high in leisure when the quality of the experience was low: thus the paradoxical situation. On the job, people feel skilful and challenged, and therefore feel more happy, strong, creative and satisfied. In their free time, people feel there is generally not much to do and their skills are not being used, and therefore they tend to feel more sad, weak, dull and dissatisfied. Yet they would like to work less and spend more time in leisure.

Why is this? It was puzzling to Csikszentmihalyi, although he speculated that the problem lies in the modern worker's relation to his or her job, that because we assume we are working out of necessity rather than choice, work time is 'perceived as time subtracted from the total time available for our life.'

He suggests that we have to get better at using our leisure. We certainly have to shatter the negative psychology surrounding the activity that makes us happiest – work.

We are learning at work; some are searching for the right job; many of us are fulfilled at work; many of us love our jobs. When we stop loving our jobs, then we often leave.

Katherine Graham, of the *Washington Post*, is quoted as saying, 'To love what you do and feel that it matters; how could anything be more fun?' The only thing that could be more fun would be to do it in a great place with people who you love. And that's happening too.

Practical techniques for controlling your thinking

An engineer has a technique and a process for building a bridge or an engine. Like an engineer, your mind also has a technique for controlling and directing your life. It is important that we realise that methods and techniques are essential to a healthy mental existence. In building a bridge, the engineer must understand mathematical principles, stresses and strains. In addition to these, he or she must have a clear picture of the finished bridge in mind. Finally, the engineer must apply tried and tested methods and principles until the bridge is built and cars drive across it. Nothing happens by chance.

Below are a number of techniques that you might consider using to keep you focused on achieving and staying positive.

Passing-over technique

This involves inducing your subconscious mind to take over your request as handed to your conscious mind. Know that your deeper mind is Infinite Intelligence and Infinite Power. Just think over what you want, and see it coming to fruition from this moment on. Be like the little boy who had a very bad cough and a sore throat. He decided firmly and repeatedly, 'It is passing away now. It is passing away now.' It passed away in about an hour. Use this technique; it is simple and works!

Your subconscious will accept your plan

If you were building a new home for yourself and your family, you know that you would be very interested with regard to the plan of your home, and you would ensure that the builders conformed to the agreed plan. You would ensure that they used the agreed materials, wood, steel, etc., all to the agreed specifications. What about your mental home and your plan for happiness, health and financial security? All the experiences that enter your life depend upon the nature of the mental building blocks that you use in the construction of your mental home.

If your thinking (plan) is full of mental patterns of fear, worry and anxiety, and if you are despondent, doubtful or cynical, then your overall thinking will become more stressed, limiting and full of tension.

The most fundamental activity in your life is what you build into your mentality every waking hour. You are building your mental home all the time, through your mental thought and imagery. Hour by hour, you build health, success and happiness by the thoughts you make, the ideas you harbour, the beliefs you accept and the scenes you rehearse in the hidden studio in your mind.

Build a new mental plan; build silently by realising that peace, happiness and goodwill are in the present moment. By dwelling on these positive states, your subconscious will accept your current thinking, and bring all these things to pass: *by their fruits ye shall know them.*

The science and art of true belief

There is a famous quotation in the Bible: 'Ask, and it will be given you. Seek, and you will find. Knock, and it will be opened for you' (Matthew 7:7).

This teaching implies the definiteness of mental and spiritual laws. It is important that you 'ask' believing if you are to receive. Your mind moves from the thought to the thing. Unless you have an image in your mind, it cannot move, for there would be nothing for it to move toward. Your want, which is a mental act, must be accepted as an image in your mind before the power of your subconscious mind will connect and work on it. You must reach a point of acceptance in your mind that is an undisputed state of agreement. The sound thinking that the science and art of true belief is the knowledge and complete confidence that the movement of your conscious mind will gain a definite response from your subconscious mind, which is one with boundless wisdom and infinite power.

By following this procedure, your wants and beliefs will be answered.

5

Being assertive

Challenges for team leaders

Strong leadership of any business should be a shared activity. To be successful you need a capable and effective management team. Teams vary in size from a few to 20 or more. There are a number of challenges that arise from time to time with most teams.

Inadequate capabilities of an individual operational leader

Sometimes an operational leader will fail to grasp the implications of their actions, such as when they deliver short-term profits by using short-sighted means that are detrimental to the values and longer-term interests that you are working for. You may have concerns about their style, such as lack of personal time management or lack of a sense of urgency. Arrogance or over-ambition may be other causes for concern.

Often the problematic person is more of a manager – competent in running the day-to-day business and an adequate staff administrator – rather than a leader. He or she lacks a strategic perspective and personal leadership and team-working skills. Such a person can manage a business but cannot grow a business. Counselling and coaching seldom do much good. Either you or your predecessor made an error in selection, and you should consider replacing an operational leader if they prove inadequate. It is never a mistake to turn back if you are on the wrong road. As a strategic leader, you are faced with some unpleasant situations and have to make tough decisions such as sacking colleagues.

Too often leaders will press ahead despite problems with individuals, instead of confronting embarrassing or awkward situations and dealing with them. This can end up in being harmful to everyone – the business, the customers, the leader, the individual and all those who work for the business.

Common team-wide shortcomings

As a leader you may have come to the conclusion that your team may not be up to the challenges (with some exceptions of course) of the competitive environment that the management team is supposed to be leading. Bringing the capabilities of your team into balance with present realities and future aspirations is a complex challenge for any strategic leader, however experienced he or she may be.

Harmful rivalries

These normally manifest as a particular rivalry between two individuals. They tend to start out as disagreements, often legitimate, over some aspect of the business, before they blossom into full-blown feuds complete with personal abuse. Sometimes, before you realise how serious it is, personal acrimony has flared out of control. Harmful rivalries are symptoms of lack of team spirit and they should never happen. A friendly rivalry between parts of the whole is natural and, within reason, should be encouraged. A tension between certain individuals can be positive rather than negative. As a leader you have to bring your team together, and encourage teamwork at every opportunity. You must go out and expect the very best communication and co-operation from all your team members, especially from your management team.

Group thinking

Cohesiveness in your team, and a degree of like-mindedness in terms of purpose and values, is essential to achieving the team's overall goals. However, you should make it clear that you expect people to voice the truth as they see it. You and others may not agree, but that is of secondary importance. To keep the group informed of actions, as well as continually measuring your team's thinking, is essential to achieving a well-maintained group cohesiveness as well as giving the business a real chance at achieving the overall goals and objectives that have been agreed by the group/team.

Fragmentation

A group of individuals is not a team. Symptoms of fragmentation include lack of co-operation between parts, failure to share information, decision-making regardless of the broad strategic direction, meetings of the management team that are perfunctory and marred by absenteeism, and the growth of separate agendas. The only person concerned or caring about the whole as opposed to the parts is *you*. If you are interested in avoiding undue stress, then remember this equation: Fragmentation = Hospitalisation.

Of course, effective leadership works towards getting the right balance of the parts and the whole of the business. Please note that fragmentation indicates that you have failed to fulfil the most essential function in your role as leader.

Dealing with emergencies and problems

Occasionally, almost miraculously, our creative potential comes forth with irresistible power and intelligence when we are in a state of emergency. To save someone she loves, a frail woman may show the courage of a tigress and the strength of a trained athlete. To avert a car accident, a driver may accomplish in a split second feat of thinking visual judgement and skill that would have taken them weeks to plot and practise. In a community emergency, flood, fire, war, etc., many ordinary men and women find themselves performing acts of genuine heroism.

Profound change

Emergencies bring about profound changes in our characters; things that may be trivial, insignificant or irrelevant drop away in an instant. Possibly you have experienced a moment of emergency in which you saw someone, perhaps yourself, accomplish a feat of muscle or mind that saved a situation, or a life.

So many good things emerge in us in an emergency. How can we produce artificially in ourselves this psycho-physical state, which permits us to use latent creative potentials without one of the major ingredients of emergency, i.e. without danger? To do this completely is impossible, but it is possible to produce a state of emergency in a measure that is efficacious without being dangerous. Our primary need is for air. Anything that prevents us from breathing threatens our life, and therefore is experienced as a major emergency.

Try this for yourself

Take a deep breath. Fill your lungs completely. Hold your breath for as long as possible, and then a little longer. Now expel the air slowly. Empty your lungs, more and more: let out the last little puff of air until you are empty. And now that you are completely empty – stay empty. Do not take in a breath – not yet – not yet – do not permit yourself to breathe, stay empty to the limit of your endurance – NOW! Let the air rush in. In those few seconds when you deliberately stop breathing, you are more or less in a state of emergency. In those eternal seconds all your 30 trillions of cells are shouting, 'Air, air, air!' For those few seconds when you were deprived of air nothing else mattered except breathing.

Now apply this lesson

Think of your present concern, question or problem (challenge); put it in a single word or name. For example:

Job, Health, Wife, Husband, Time, Loneliness, Money, Pain

The word or name represents your thoughts or feelings about a state of affairs that is disturbing you. Here is a sequence to try; practise it lying down:

- in a single word or name, express your question, concern or problem;

- mentally repeating that word, fill your lungs to their maximum capacity;

- mentally repeating that word, keep the air in your lungs for as long as you can comfortably;

- mentally repeating that word, slowly let the air come through your mouth – all of it;

- mentally repeating that word, make sure there is no more air in you; expel the last of it by sounding the letter 'ess' for as long as you can;

- mentally repeating the word, pull in your abdomen and hold the muscles tight;

- be watchful – the natural tendency is to take a breath through your nose without being aware of it;

- mentally repeating the word, remain empty and without motion for as long as you can – as your cells cry out for air, keep repeating that word – when you cannot hold out any longer – breathe! Let the longed-for air flow into you like a river of luminous energy, revitalising every cell of your body.

What's the point of all this?

Well here are a few of the things that can happen.

In the context of a life-and-death emergency, your problem will in all probability change in proportion. By focusing on your problem in such a way you set your subconscious mind to work on it. Thus, you may gain a completely new view on it from your deep mind.

The physiological effect of this kind of breathing, combined with the psychological approach, is very powerful. You will feel an increased mental activity and vigour, a physical exhilaration, a renewal of life flowing into you. You will become aware that the ordinary automatic process of breathing can be transformed into a most wonderful, conscious act.

Just try it!

Even for those who have no problem, this is an excellent exercise. Try it!

This is a powerful exercise, but do not overdo it. If you have, or suspect you have, any weakness of heart or lungs, consult your doctor.

You can achieve anything if you apply new strategies and new ways.

Improving your relationships

We tend to be at our most unrealistic when looking at what went wrong in failed relationships. This is probably because they are so important to us and we have invested in them. If you want to change, or develop new ways in which to relate to others, then you will have to start with a good dose of reality. Here are some guidelines to help you focus on what is realistic.

Work on changing yourself

The temptation in stormy relationships is to think that it is the other person who needs to change. It may be true that the other person should change, but as you cannot change the other person, it is often a complete waste of time and effort in trying. The best way to change the other person is to change yourself – to change the way in which you relate to them. Working to change yourself is often a real challenge.

Do not be distracted in attempts to change others: change yourself and change the way you relate to others. Leave these changes to them, and the relationship will feel better for you both.

Changes take time

When you change the way in which you relate to others, they may resist that change and try to make you change back. So making changes in relationships can take longer than making changes in yourself alone, and it certainly requires persistence.

Work with people and accept them

When you find yourself saying, 'If only she would tell me what she's thinking' or 'If only he didn't criticise me so much', stop yourself and remind yourself to be realistic. If you want to bring about some changes in those relationships, you should stop thinking 'if only' and accept people as they are. Once you start to make changes in yourself, the other person is also likely to begin to change. Then you will be able to find out if you can accommodate each other and get on.

If after you have tried to change you still find the relationship is no better, and you keep wishing the other person were different, then it might be better to end the relationship.

In addition to the above, there are other strategies you can try.

- Be assertive with people; let them know what you are thinking and feeling, and be fair with them.

- Understand the voices from the past. When we recognise these voices, and learn how to think about them, we can choose to ignore them or choose to listen to other voices instead. If we fail to recognise them, they can cause havoc within our relationships.

- Understand that relationships are systems. When we make changes in the ways we relate to others, those others will tend to respond to, and resist, the changes. In a system, one change leads to another, and the skills of communication and negotiation help to ensure that the changes that we want and that others want match – the system (relationship) can adjust and adapt.

Being more assertive

Assertiveness is like a language, just as learning a language helps you to get to know, and to like, French or German people for example. Assertiveness is much like learning a language, or learning how to use a tool, that facilitates communication and understanding. Like a language, it has different facets and uses, and involves many different skills. Here are some of the ways that you can build your assertiveness skills.

Listen to others

Think about the behaviour of aggressive people who make demands without having any regard for what others think. Instead of succeeding in the attempt to dominate others, these people often put themselves in a weaker, more vulnerable position and fail to listen. Listening carefully to what someone is saying means giving your undivided attention. A good listener will understand the words said, but will also be able to pick up on how the person is feeling. You may need to verify whether your guess is right: 'You seem really worried about that,' or 'You sound extremely irritable to me.'

Guidelines to effective listening

- Look at the person speaking, nod and give verbal signals, e.g. 'uh-huh.'
- Reflect, or repeat back a few words: 'You were tired', 'You didn't?'
- Summarise to show you understood, e.g. 'They asked you to take over.'
- When you agree, say so.
- Listen for what people mean by what they say, or what they don't say.
- Listen to the end. There may be a twist in the tail of the message.
- Take off your blinkers and don't jump to conclusions. Be a support to others; sometimes they don't want you to solve their problems, but they do want you to *listen*.

Use the 'unselfish I'

To say 'I want to be home by six o'clock' is being fair to yourself if that is what you want; it is not being selfish. It is only fair to express yourself clearly, especially when you want something. There is no need to beat about the bush, nor to be vague, coy or embarrassed. If others have the right to speak up for themselves, to express themselves and expect their viewpoint to be respected, then so do you. Accept your feelings for what they are and not as if taking account of them makes you selfish. If you feel angry, then that is how you feel. There is little point in telling yourself you *should not* be angry. Acknowledge the feeling, so that you can express it or manage it appropriately.

Stick to the important points

Have you heard of the 'ten leaky buckets argument'? This means putting forward many weak arguments in the hope that together they will add up to one good one – which of course they never will. What you want is one watertight bucket, not ten leaky ones. In reality, many leaky buckets actually weaken a good case. Leaky arguments turn your whole case into excuses rather than arguments. An example of this might be that you have been invited to an event that you don't want to attend, so you make a weak excuse that you have to do something else, which comes across as being unconvincing, where sometimes it is much better to say, 'Thanks for the invite, but I have too much going on just now, but thanks for asking.' There is no comeback on this. You have stated your decision and given a single clear reason. If your answer is not accepted, then repeat the message, either by just repeating the same words, or slightly differently: 'No, I'm afraid I can't,' 'I'm sorry, but I am too busy', 'It sounds great, but I can't.'

Sticking to important points

Step 1 – decide what you want

Step 2 – express this clearly

Step 3 – think of as many other ways of expressing your decision as you can

Try the three-step technique in some of the following situations: refuse to look after someone's pet while they are away on holiday; ask for your money back; change some theatre tickets; turn down an invitation or date; get your children to clean their bedrooms.

Saying 'no' nicely

If someone asks you to do something you don't want to do, then all you have to do is say no. You are under no obligation to explain yourself. Here are a few phrases that will help you say no without causing offence:

- show appreciation first – 'Thank you for asking me', 'That's nice of you.'

- acknowledge the person asking – 'I know that it is important to you.'

- give a clear reason for refusing – 'I am already committed to ...'

- help the other person by suggesting someone else they can ask instead.

The sleep on it rule

If in any doubt, never commit yourself until the next day at the earliest. It gives you time to think. This rule can save many regrets later.

Some rules of perspective – dealing with problems

Having a problem can dominate your life. Whichever way you turn, the mountain or the cliff edge looms ahead, providing a dispiriting or alarming perspective. The following ideas may be helpful when trying to find the most useful perspective.

1. The 100-Year Rule – will it matter in 100 years? Will anyone even remember what the problem was? Of course, this is something of an exaggeration, as none of us will be here in 100 years. It is meant as a reminder that those things that seem hugely important today may matter little when seen from a great distance. When you stand beside an elephant, it is extremely hard to see anything else. When you step back from it, the rest of the animal kingdom, the other visitors to the zoo and their surroundings all come into view.

2. The Measuring Rod Rule – is the problem that is bothering you really the most important thing in your life at the moment? Imagine that you have an important job to do today. You feel tense and worried about it, and the traffic jam on the way to work is enough to send you into a tirade of anger against all the bad drivers on the road. Of course, the traffic jam is important to you, but only as an impediment, only as something that gets in the way of doing something that is of far greater importance in the long term.

3. The Middle of the Night Rule – in the early hours of the morning, when you lie awake, problems (challenges) and worries can seem insurmountable. In the cool light of day, they can be more truly seen for what they are – molehills rather than mountains. The rule is: think about them in the morning or during the day. It is always difficult to keep things in perspective when lying awake worrying at night. Tell yourself, 'This is not the time.'

4. The 'Water-under-the-bridge' Rule or Statute of Limitations – you feel bad about things you did, or things

you did not do. They continue to trouble you long past the time when they should. Let them flow by you instead, and look back on them as if they were someone else's mistakes or troubles. You may be carrying an unnecessary load, weighing yourself down with matters that are well past their sell-by date. There comes a time when you have punished yourself enough.

Remember, there is always more than one way of seeing things.

This means that although you may not be able to choose the facts, you may be able to choose how you react to them, and help yourself feel better and act more effectively by looking at them differently. The methods described above reveal how your feelings and thoughts are linked, and how these thoughts and feelings colour your mood. If you practise them, you will discover the kind of thinking that helps you feel good. When practising them, it is useful to ask yourself questions, e.g. 'Is there another way of seeing things?'

Step 1 – recognise your thoughts and the way your thoughts and moods link together. The following questions are worth considering:

- what went through my mind at the time?
- how am I seeing things now?
- what is it about this that matters to me?
- what does this event or situation mean to me?

Step 2 – re-examine your thoughts. You will find that there are many perspectives from which you can look at a situation. Finding new perspectives gives you more options and helps you feel better. The following questions are worth considering.

1. Questions about thoughts:
   - what other points of view are there?
   - how would someone else think about this?
   - how else could I think about it?
   - how would I think about this if I were feeling better?
2. Questions about reality:
   - what are the facts of the case?
   - how can I find out which way of thinking fits the facts best?
   - what is the evidence?
3. Questions about your thinking:
   - could I be making a mistake in the way I am thinking?
   - am I pressurising myself?
   - am I using the language of an extremist?
4. Questions about coping:
   - what is the worst that could happen?
   - how bad is this going to get?
   - what can I do when that happens?
   - how can I get help?

Strategies to help you when making decisions

It is very rare for most of us to make 'perfect decisions' every time. Every course of action will lead to more choices and will throw up some unexpected difficulties. The following strategies should help you in making difficult decisions, but if you become too worried in the pursuit of the perfect decision, you will be more likely to become painfully indecisive.

The balance sheet

Divide a piece of paper down the middle and add two headings: advantages and disadvantages. Write the specific question you are thinking about at the top of the page, e.g. Shall I expand the business now?, Shall I book a summer holiday? Shall I go on Ian Hunt's management course? Then fill in the columns, considering the situation from all its aspects: how it affects others as well as yourself, including its implications and consequences. Think of factors that are important in both the long and the short term. This exercise is done best on paper as it is difficult to hold all the ideas in one's mind at once. Now look through the list and weigh up the balance. Some items will count more than others. It is helpful to give points out of 10 to each advantage and disadvantage, according to how important they are, and then to add the columns separately, e.g. 69 for and 34 against. It might help if there are many advantages and disadvantages to decide the two most significant in each column and weigh them against each other without being distracted by relatively unimportant considerations.

Trial runs and time protection

If you are having difficulty in making a choice – e.g. whether or not to move house – pretend that you have made a choice (to move) and then imagine, as fully as possible, what it would be like had that choice been made. Does it feel right? With important decisions that are not urgent, imagine 'living' that choice for several days, and then imagine the other choice. This exercise gives you an opportunity to take yourself through a trial run and to make contact with your 'gut' reaction. You may then know what to do, but if not, you can go back to your balance sheet and think whether other points need adding.

Another way of doing this is to make use of 'time protection.' This is a simple strategy that involves imagining yourself at some future date ahead, six months, one year, five years, etc., having made the decision that you are now finding difficult. From your new vantage point, look back to the present, and at the decision that you are trying to make. You may immediately find it easier to make up your mind, or you may wish to imagine taking different options in turn until you find the one you like best.

A sounding board

Other people can provide a useful sounding board, and may reflect back to you their understanding of your problem and of your inclinations. Ask up to three people whom you trust and then 'make up your mind' is a useful guiding principle that should lead to a considered decision. The nature of the problem will help you to decide the best people to consult. If it is a specialist subject then talking to someone who is 'up to speed' on the subject is recommended, e.g. with a major financial decision, you should perhaps consult an accountant, a bank manager or a financial advisor. Perhaps you should visit the library and search for relevant information or consult the internet on a specific subject.

Information gathering and sifting

If you were choosing a new car, and safety is an important consideration, then you need information about the safety features of different cars. Before making such decisions, it is important to clarify those factors that are significant to you and for which you need more information. Once you have listed these factors, you can think about how to find the necessary information. Research tells us that decision-making improves with practice. In order to make effective decisions, inexperienced people need both to be trained in the use of relevant information systems and to be given practice in making decisions. Otherwise, they will be more likely to make mistakes.

Dealing with chain reactions

Often decisions hang together. Douglas wanted a new job, but his wife, Mary, was happy with the one she had. They discussed the options first, and made the decision that Douglas would try and get a new job nearby, but that if he failed, then Mary would think about making changes herself. As things transpired, Douglas found an exciting new opportunity, but it was a three-hour drive away – an impossible commute. A chain reaction of decisions was set in motion. They concentrated on making these decisions in the most sensible order for them. First, they discussed whether to work in different places, and decided they wanted to continue living together. Then, Mary decided to look for a new job. She was uncertain how to proceed, so she consulted a colleague, and with her advice in mind, spoke to her boss before starting the search for new jobs. One job, less interesting to her, started immediately; another would not begin for six months. She and Douglas now had to decide when to sell their house, and when and where to look for another one. All options seemed to involve them in financial strain (renting temporary accommodation, storing of belongings, etc.) and every decision seemed important. For each aspect of the problem they could specify, they balanced up the relative advantages. They then made the best decisions they could. Having first given their attention to the series of big changes in their lives, they were then able to tackle the host of minor ones that followed – whether to sell the old sofa, how to transport their belongings, etc.

Keeping up your energy reserves

Logically, you should spend more time and energy on big decisions than on smaller ones. Lengthy deliberations on whether to wear your blue tie or your black tie, or whether to buy the giant size pack of soap powder, or which traffic line to join make little sense. However, not doing so is harder in practice than in theory. The first interfering factor is fatigue. Being tired can make it difficult to make even the simplest of decisions. Preoccupation is the second interfering factor. People whose energies are necessarily devoted to important and worrying decisions, such as whether to close the business, whether to have major surgery or whether get a divorce, frequently find the smaller decisions especially difficult and intrusive, as if their reserves are already depleted, and they have little attention for anything else. It helps then to ask yourself, 'How much does it really matter?' Next, turn as many small decisions into routines as you possibly can, and leave those of even lesser importance for later or for others.

Give something for nothing

In the business world, most of our giving is to get something in return, although not necessarily of the same kind or from the same person. Often we calculate the return, realistically or not, as the case may be. Often we expect lifelong gratitude or special recognition for what we have given or done. Often we are disappointed or disillusioned as the return is nothing like what we anticipated. What happens when your response is less than I thought I have a right to expect? I am angry or hurt; I feel that I am a victim of your thoughtlessness, or the world's. I feel unrecognised, undervalued; I am pained and embittered. I think, 'Look at all I have given, and what do I get? Nothing.'

This sort of giving is not giving, but trading. When we think of it as giving we are bound to suffer disappointment, and the painful, harmful feelings that go with this disappointment.

The other sort of giving is the giving itself. It has no strings attached, no expectations either open or concealed. The person who gives for the pleasure he or she gets out of giving is usually satisfied and happy with the act itself. The act of giving is its own reward. If something comes in return, it is an unanticipated piece of good luck. The following technique asks you to perform, voluntarily, consciously, the act of giving something for nothing. Here are the preparatory steps to giving something for nothing.

Recognise the difference between:

- giving something with the conscious or unconscious expectation of being paid back, and

- voluntarily giving something without expecting a return.

Ask yourself: Have I in the past given something and received nothing? Did I feel cheated? Was I giving in order to get, or was I genuinely giving something for nothing? If I really intended to give something for nothing, why did I resent getting nothing in return?

Recognise your feelings as you set out voluntarily to give something for nothing.

- Do you like yourself? Then like yourself.

- Do you feel like a fool? Then feel like a fool.

- Are you furious at a situation or person? Then be furious.

- Recognise that you are setting out to achieve the impossible. Go out and do it. Freely and voluntarily give something for nothing.

The choice is vast. Do not strain too much in maintaining anonymity, or in trying to find someone who will not appreciate your giving. In other words, do not strain too much to get nothing out of giving – it is impossible. For you to get nothing out of giving – it is impossible. For you will get something, somehow, if not from others then from yourself. So do not think too much; lightly and nonchalantly – *give something for nothing*.

Here are a list of possibilities for the impossible task of giving something for nothing:

- bring a flower to someone who never receives them;
- ask someone's opinion about a subject he or she knows very well;
- take someone to the theatre or cinema;
- anticipate someone's needs and take care of it;
- help an in-law, without strings;
- let your parent help you, in his or her way not in yours;
- cook someone his or her favourite meal;
- let your child help you, in his or her way not in yours;
- call up a lonely person;
- give a specific thoughtful compliment;
- let someone talk to you for two hours – never say the pronoun 'I';
- clean someone's shoes.

Add to this list: *You can achieve anything if you apply new strategies, new ways*!

How to hold productive meetings

There are a number of tried and tested ways for making every meeting more productive and time effective.

Set clear goals. Ask what purpose will be served by this meeting? Is it to:

- Make a decision?
- Analyse or solve a problem?
- Provide the group with new information?
- Gather data about the state of a particular project?

Be clear in your own mind exactly what outcome you are aiming to achieve. Write this as a single-line mission statement and place it in clear view of all those attending – use a flipchart, placed within easy reach.

1. *Provide everyone with a written agenda.* All meetings should have a written agenda. This should be circulated as far in advance of the meeting as is realistically possible, to allow those attending time to prepare. Ask yourself what you want to emerge from the meeting. What changes in attitudes are you looking for? Explain your agenda at the start of the meeting, then move directly to the main purpose.

2. *Keep the number present to a minimum.* Invite only those who need to be there. Calculate the cost of the meeting – based on the wages and overheads of all those present – then write this up on the flipchart below your mission statement.

3. *Avoid on-the-hour starts.* My experience is that people are more likely to be punctual when attending meetings that are held off the hour. More people arrive late for a meeting scheduled to start at 10 a.m. for example than

for one which begins at 10.15 a.m. You should also set a finishing time for the meeting and stick to it.

4. *If the agenda is brief, keep everyone standing.* This tactic offers two benefits:

   - people are more alert when standing than when seated and are less likely to miss important points;
   - nobody wants needlessly to prolong the meeting, so the agenda can be worked through far faster and more efficiently.

5. *Use the 'talking ball' technique.* This technique was pioneered by Texas Instruments, and involves passing a rubber ball around the group, only the person actually holding it being allowed to speak. This saves time by preventing the speaker being needlessly interrupted.

6. *Take regular straw polls to check consensus.* People sometimes talk more to air their views than to resolve conflicts. Prevent this by taking informal polls from time to time to assess consensus. If there is general agreement on a course of action, it can be put to the meeting instantly for a formal vote, instead of wasting time on unnecessary debate.

7. *Try the Japanese technique of Nemawashi.* This can be a major time saver. It involves bringing together small groups of specialists for brief discussions prior to one or two of them attending the meeting. The idea is a sound one and has been widely implemented. It saves time by allowing the specialist to make immediate decisions instead of referring the matter back every so often.

8. *Keep everybody focused.* One way of doing this is to calculate the cost of the meeting, i.e. the wage bill of everyone attending and write this in large letters on the flipchart. When people realise how much each

irrelevance costs, even the most determined side-tracker tends to hold his or her tongue.

9. *Prevent one-to-one discussions.* If two participants lock horns and begin to discuss an issue between them, excluding the rest of the group, immediately reschedule the issue as a meeting between just those two protagonists. Then firmly call their attention back to the purpose of the present meeting.

10. *Arouse interest through careful planning.* Exert a positive influence over the attitudes and expectations of those attending by:

    – obliging everyone to prepare for the meeting, e.g. you might insist that everyone will give a five-minute presentation on their progress since the last meeting;

    – during the meeting, select speakers at random;

    – make everyone present feel their involvement is valued and that important information can be gained from the session.

11. *End with a call for action.* Encourage those attending the meeting to take some clear action as a result of the meeting, by making it clear you intend to follow-up on what was agreed. Then do so!

Effective delegation

For many managers, the greatest failure of time management lies in their inability or reluctance to delegate. Research suggests that, in some companies, as much as 95% of a manager's day is spent not in managing but in doing. One study found that half of all managerial time was occupied by work that would have been more efficiently carried out by secretaries, and over 40% was taken up by tasks that should have been delegated to colleagues or team members. As a result, only 5% was devoted to activities the managers were uniquely qualified to perform. Delegation enables you to spend more time on what you do well and less on what you do less well. All successful managers recognise that effective delegation is essential for efficient time management.

Psychological barriers to delegation

Why then are so many reluctant to delegate even the most routine tasks? The answer can usually be found in three psychological barriers:

- *Fear of surrendering their authority.* Some managers worry that by delegating anything but the most trivial jobs they will weaken their standing in the organisation. The truth is that by delegating responsible tasks, and growth-enhancing tasks, team members become more efficient, motivated and productive. As a result, the manager who is good at delegating enjoys greater authority and status within the organisation.

- *Fear that mistakes will be made.* This usually arises from a lack of confidence in either themselves and/or their team members. Although mistakes will always be made, this risk will be significantly reduced through appropriate delegation (see below) and careful monitoring of progress.

- *Fear of the invisible.* Some managers prefer to keep a tight hold on key assignments in the belief that this ensures a high profile within the business. However, because team members are therefore never groomed for promotion, the manager's own chances of advancement are diminished. There are no sufficiently experienced subordinates to take over his or her responsibilities.

Faulty delegation

This occurs when:

- a team member does not understand and/or is incapable of carrying out the task;

- instructions are repeated many times before the task is completed correctly;

- the work is carried out incorrectly and has to be redone – either by the team member or by the delegating manager;

- the team member lacks sufficient motivation to do the work properly.

Six tasks you should never delegate

If you are a manager, there are only six tasks that should never to be delegated:

- planning a key project
- selecting the team for that project
- monitoring the team's efforts
- motivating team members
- evaluating team members
- rewarding team members

Almost everything else you do could probably be delegated.

When and what to delegate

- When a job can be done satisfactorily by someone earning less than yourself – or less than you aspire to earn.

Tasks which can be delegated include:

reorganising files;

taking unnecessary telephone calls;

fitting a fuse on a desk lamp, overhead projector, etc.;

typing a memo, letter, report, etc.;

taking letters to the post.

- When you lack the necessary skill, knowledge or experience to do the task.

  Refuse to become involved in such tasks. Attempting to do them wastes time and often produces a job so botched that it has to be corrected by an expert.

- When the task is routine.

  They may waste your time in small amounts, five minutes here, ten minutes there, but the total daily and weekly loss is significant. Tasks which can't be delegated to a team member, can, thanks to technology, often be delegated to machinery.

- When the task helps team members to grow.

  These are challenges that will help your team members to grow by mastering new skills and gaining greater expertise. By delegating such tasks whenever possible, you not only save yourself time but enable others to enhance their skills, so taking even more burden off your shoulders in the months to come.

Making and keeping commitments

At the heart of our overall well-being is our ability to make and keep commitments and promises. The commitments we make to ourselves and others, and our integrity to those commitments, is the essence and clearest evidence to our proactivity. It is also the key to our overall growth. Through our human endowments of self-awareness and conscience, we become conscious of areas of weakness, areas for improvement, areas of talent that could be developed, and areas that need to be changed or eliminated from our lives. Then, as we recognise and use our imagination and independent will to act on that awareness – making promises, setting goals and being true to them – we build the strength of character, the being, that makes possible every other positive thing in our lives.

It is here we find two ways to put ourselves in control of our lives immediately. We can make a promise – and keep it. Or we can set a goal – and work to achieve it. As we make and keep commitments, even small commitments, we begin to establish an inner integrity that gives us the awareness of self-control and the courage and strength to accept more of the responsibility for our own lives.

The power to make and keep commitments to ourselves is the essence of developing the basic habits of effectiveness. Knowledge, skill and desire are all within our control. We can work on any one to improve the balance of the three. As the area of intersection becomes larger, we more deeply internalise the principles upon which habits are based and create the strength of character to move us in a balanced way toward increasing effectiveness in our lives.

Proactivity: the 30-day test

It is in the ordinary events of every day that we develop the proactive capacity to handle the extraordinary pressures of life. It's how we make and keep commitments, how we handle a traffic jam, how we respond to an irate customer or a disobedient child. It's how we view our problems (challenges) and where we focus our energies. It's the language we use.

I challenge you to test your proactivity for 30 days. Simply try it and see what happens. For 30 days work only with your circle of influence. Make small commitments and keep them.

- Be the light, not the judge.
- Be a model not a critic.
- Be part of the solution, not part of the problem.

Try it in your marriage, in your family, in your job; don't argue for other people's weaknesses. Don't argue for your own. When you make a mistake, admit it, correct it and learn from it – immediately. Don't get into a blaming, accusing mode. Work on things you have control over. Work on you and on being the best you can be!

Look at weaknesses of others with compassion, not accusation. It's not what they're not doing or should be doing that's the issue. The issue is your own chosen response to the situation and what you should be doing. If you start to think the problem is 'out there', stop yourself. That thought is a problem.

People who exercise their embryonic freedom day after day will, gradually, expand their freedom. People who do not, find that it withers until they are literally 'being lived.' They are acting out the scripts written by parents, associates and society.

We are responsible for our own effectiveness, for our own happiness and ultimately, I would say, for most of our circumstances.

Samuel Johnson observed, 'The fountain of content must spring up in the mind, and he who hath so little knowledge of human nature as to seek happiness by changing anything but his own disposition, will waste his life in fruitless efforts and multiply grief he proposes to remove.'

Knowing that we are responsible, 'response – able', is fundamental to effectiveness and to every other habit of effectiveness I will discuss.

Making an impact with people you meet

Actions speak louder than words, and a smile says, 'I like you. You make me happy. I am glad to see you.'

The ancient Chinese were wise – wise in the ways of the world; and they had a proverb that you and I should cut out and paste inside our diaries: 'A man without a smiling face must not open a shop.'

Your smile is a messenger of goodwill. Your smile brightens the lives of all who see it. To someone who has seen a dozen people frown, scowl or turn their faces away, your smile is like the sun breaking through the clouds, especially when that someone is under pressure from his or her boss, customers, children, relatives, etc. A smile can help them realise that all is not hopeless – that there is joy in the world.

Some years ago, a department store in New York, in recognition of the pressures its sales clerks were under during the Christmas rush, presented the readers of its advertisements with the following homely philosophy:

The value of a smile at Christmas (or anytime really)
It costs nothing, but creates much.
It enriches those who receive, without impoverishing those who give.

It happens in a flash and the memory of it sometimes lasts forever.

None are so rich they can get along without it, and none so poor but are richer for all its benefits.

It creates happiness in the home, fosters goodwill in a business, and is the countersign of friends.

It is rest to the weary, daylight to the discouraged, sunshine to the sad, and Nature's best antidote for trouble.

Yet it cannot be bought, begged, borrowed, or stolen, for it is something that is no earthly good to anybody till it is given away.

And if in the last-minute rush of Christmas buying some of our salespeople should be too tired to give you a smile, may we ask you to leave one of yours?

For nobody needs a smile so much as those who have none left to give.

Say no when you haven't the knowledge or skills

Many people make a fundamental mistake when they 'have a go' at a job for which they lack the necessary knowledge or qualification. They do so sometimes just to show willing. Sometimes this can result in you wasting your time and other people's time as well. Here are some examples:

- 'The photocopier has gone wrong again. Could you take a look at it for me?'

- 'I can't get my car to start. Could you get it going?'

- 'I'm not sure how to run this spreadsheet on the computer. Can you give me a hand?'

Unless you are a expert on copiers, cars or spreadsheets, the most sensible thing to do is decline politely. Men are more likely to fall into this situation, as they are reluctant to admit ignorance of anything mechanical/technical. If you don't know, then refuse to be drawn into playing Boy Scout or Girl Guide.

If you are forced into the situation of having to have a look, then here is a simple checklist of what to consider:

- is the equipment plugged in?
- is it switched on?
- has a fuse blown?
- is there an easily cleared paper jam in the photocopier?
- have you removed the protective plastic strip from the toner?

Providing an easily followed flow chart, which enables even a complete novice to sort out minor problems, and providing clear guidance on when to send for an expert can be a great time saver.

Another approach, which was used in an American office computer department, uses humour to convey the message:

If you don't understand, don't interfere

The department manager claimed that his notice, reproduced below, had reduced time wasted through inexpert fiddling with his technology. He said that it deterred even senior management from messing about with the equipment, without upsetting anyone. Why not try it for yourself and see.

AUCHTUNG ALLES LOOKENSPEEPERS
DAS COMPUTERMACHINE IS NICHT FUER GEFINGER-POKEN
UND MIITTENGRABBEN. IST EASY SCHNAPPEN DER

SPRINGENWERK, BLOWENFUSEN UND POPPENCORKEN MIT SPITZENPARKEN. IST NICHT FUER GEWERKEN BEI DAS DUMPKOPFEN. DAS RUBBERNECKEN SIGHTSEEREN KEEPEN DAS COTTENPICKEN HANS IN DAS POCKETS MUSS; RELAXEN UND WATCHEN DAS BLINKENLICHTEN.

Saying 'no' when the task need not be done at all

Consider all tasks before embarking on them. Ask yourself:

- Does doing this bring me closer to my goal?
- If not, why do I have to spend time on it?
- If I decide not to do it, what negative consequences are likely to follow?

Whether or not it can be dropped depends on who made the request or gave the instruction. When the instruction comes from your boss, you may have no option but to go along with it. When negotiating your reason for not doing the task, demonstrating the financial cost sometimes leads to a rethink. On other occasions there will be nothing for it but to grit your teeth and get on with it. If such demands are a frequent occurrence, build a margin for these 'time-bandit' activities into your schedule.

How to get the results you want

The two principal reasons for failure are having a lack of confidence and trying too hard. Many people block answers to their prayers by failing to understand the workings of their subconscious mind. Whenever your subconscious mind accepts an idea, it immediately begins to execute it. It uses all its mighty resources to that end and mobilises all the mental and spiritual laws of your deeper mind. This law is true for good and bad ideas. Consequently, if you use it negatively, it brings trouble, failure and confusion. When you use it constructively, it brings guidance, freedom and peace of mind. The right answer is inevitable when your thoughts are positive, constructive and loving. The only thing that you have to do in order to overcome failure is to persuade your subconscious mind to accept your idea or request by feeling its reality now, and the law of your mind will do the rest. If you request with faith and confidence your subconscious mind will come up with answers for you.

To believe is to accept something is true, or to live in the state of being it. If you sustain this thinking, you will almost certainly experience the joy of achieving what you believe. There are three steps to success in this regard:

1. Take a look at the problem.

2. Turn to the solution or way out known only to the subconscious mind.

3. Rest in the sense of deep conviction that it is done.

Do not weaken your thinking by saying, 'I wish I could believe' or 'I hope so.' Your feelings have to be sincere and positive, you have to control your feelings, you have to be 'the boss.' Harmony is yours. Pass on the perceived problem to your subconscious mind to the point of conviction, then relax.

By relaxation, you impress your subconscious mind, enabling the kinetic energy behind the idea to take over and bring about concrete realisation.

Coue, the famous French psychologist, defined the law of reversed effort: 'When your desires and imagination are in conflict, your imagination invariably gains the day.' An example of this would be if you were asked to walk a plank on the floor, this would present little problem. However, if the plank were to be placed 20 feet up in the air between two walls, would you still walk along it?

Some people would find that their desire, will or effort to walk along the plank would be reversed, and the dominant idea of failure would be reinforced.

To avoid conflict between desires and imagination, you should enter into a drowsy state, either before sleeping or before waking up fully. The best time to impregnate your subconscious is prior to sleep. The reason for this is that the highest degree of outcropping of the subconscious occurs prior to sleep and after we waken. In this state, the negative thoughts and imagery that tend to neutralise your desire and so prevent acceptance by your subconscious mind no longer present themselves.

When you imagine the reality of the fulfilled desire and feel the thrill of accomplishment, your subconscious brings about the realisation of your desire.

A great number of people solve all their dilemmas and challenges by the play of their controlled, directed and disciplined imagination, knowing that whatever they imagine and feel is true *will* and *must* come to pass.

Remember, you can avoid conflict between conscious and subconscious in the sleepy state. Imagine the fulfilment of your desire over and over again prior to sleep. Sleep in peace and wake in joy!

6

Building a team

How to coach your people

You may be required to take on a coaching role in one of a number of circumstances:

- line managers are not fully trained in coaching skills and seek your assistance in the coaching of their team;

- line managers have insufficient time to devote to coaching of their team, particularly when their teams are very large or when their teams are geographically widespread;

- a number of key individuals need to develop a new set of skills, knowledge or behaviours and there are no appropriate training courses available;

- to follow up a particular training event with individuals who feel they need additional assistance;

- to support e-learning initiatives should individuals require particular assistance.

Personal coaching

This is when you coach on a one-to-one basis with someone over a specific time-frame. A personal trainer will work with an individual to design a programme that helps focus on their specific needs. This may be job related only or linked to the broader aspects of their life. The initial meeting will work on setting SMART goals and subsequent meetings will help the individual measure their progress against these goals.

Typically the areas covered may relate to personal ambitions, work-related opportunities or the achievement of a work/life balance where the individual needs additional focus to help them make significant progress.

It is important to establish your own personal code of practice. For example:

- respect confidentiality at all times;
- respond by coaching not counselling;
- work to create a supportive and appropriately challenging environment;
- be prepared to build an enduring relationship with the learner;
- have the desire to want to model and challenge your own development;
- be curious, and stimulate curiosity in your learner;
- recognise that the individual is in charge of his or her own destiny.

Using coaching skills

In each of the potential coaching situations described above the coach should follow the following guidelines:

- find time and place to devote full, uninterrupted attention to the learner who is being coached;
- give praise whenever possible in building the relationship;
- be honest;

- use questioning and listening techniques/skills to help the learner identify situations where they need support and new requirements for skills, knowledge and behaviours;

- be aware of body language and any other signs which demonstrate that the learner is having difficulties with the coaching – be prepared to try a different approach;

- clarify the points discussed and, when appropriate, note the agreed plans of action;

- ensure the dates and times of the next coaching sessions are agreed – coaching should be a continuous activity;

- recognise when further formal training is required in addition to the current coaching.

Coaches should try to think how their style of coaching will match with the learner's style, or preferred learning style. The coach should adopt a supportive, encouraging style. Be ready to evaluate each coaching session and your overall coaching programme.

Checklist for using coaching skills

- Have the coach and the learner agreed the overall goals of the coaching?

- Is the coach skilled in questioning, listening and feedback techniques?

- Are notes taken and shared?

- How will the effectiveness of the coaching be judged?

- How can the coaching style and skills be improved?

- Does the coach use each coaching session as a personal learning experience to review what went well and what could be better?

Key functions of effective leadership

In his book *Effective Strategic Leadership*, John Adair plots a checklist of the main ways of being an effective leader, under six main headings: planning, initiating, controlling, supporting, informing and evaluating.

Under each heading are a number of actions that he suggests to help you to carry out each specific function.

Planning

- Seeking out all available information
- Defining the group task, purpose and goal
- Making a workable plan (in the right decision-making framework)

Initiating

- Briefing the team on the aims and the plan
- Explaining why the aim or plan is necessary
- Allocating tasks to group members
- Selling team standards

Controlling

- Maintaining group standards
- Influencing tempo
- Ensuring all actions are taken towards objectives
- Keeping discussion relevant
- Prodding the group to action/decision

Supporting

- Expressing acceptance of persons and their contribution
- Encouraging team/individuals
- Disciplining team/individuals
- Creating team spirit
- Relieving tension with humour
- Reconciling disagreements or getting others to explore them

Informing

- Clarifying task and play
- Giving new information to the group – keeping them 'in the picture'
- Receiving information from the group
- Summarising suggestions and ideas coherently

Evaluating

- Checking feasibility
- Testing the consequences of the proposed solution
- Evaluating team performance
- Helping the team or an individual to evaluate their own performance against standards

In summary, a leader is the sort of person with the appropriate qualities and knowledge – which is more than technical or professional – who is able to provide the necessary functions to enable a team to achieve its task and to hold it together as a working unity. The leader must do this by eliciting the contributions and willing co-operation of all those involved.

Sir John Smyth, VC, wrote:

> A good leader is someone whom people will follow through thick and thin, in good times and in bad, because they have confidence in him or her as a person, his/her ability and his/her knowledge of the job and because they know that they matter to him/her.

How to motivate your people

Here are a number of strategies to help you motivate your people. Take the following ideas and adapt them to fit into your own philosophy of life.

Be prepared to trust others

Most of us have had experiences where we have trusted others and have been let down. It is tempting to say to oneself, 'never again.' However, in the long term, the benefits of trusting others far outweigh the tactical reverses that constitute such experiences. Of course, some individuals are less trustworthy than others, and it would foolish to trust them without safeguards. Some say that it is a vice to trust all, but equally it is a vice not to trust at all. It is having the feeling that a person will not fail in any situation that calls for dependability, discretion or fairness. Such trust may be justified or misguided, so why recommend trusting people as a general rule?

The argument for is a subjective one. I know that I respond positively if another person trusts me and negatively if they seem to regard me as untrustworthy.

'Those who trust us, educate us', said George Eliot. To educate, related to the latin verb *educere*, to lead out and to educe means to draw out something hidden, latent or reserved. Trust does elicit our inner human resource. 'Trust men and they will be true to you', declared Emerson; 'Treat them greatly and they will show themselves great.'

'Love everyone'

Love carries overtones of strong positive emotion about someone or something, and there are different kinds and degrees of love. 'Do wrong to none' is one basic principle of love. Paradoxically, you can love someone without liking him or her as an individual. If refraining from doing them wrong – which is very hard if wrong has been done to you – is the basement of love, then the first floor is everyday sympathy and kindness.

No one can be a great leader unless they can love their team members, just as no one can be described as a good parent who does wrong to their children, or withholds human warmth, sympathy and kindness. This principle applies to all those with whom we work, whether in less structured ways in self-employment, in involvement with the community or within the company workplace.

Act with integrity

This means that you are giving others grounds to trust you: you do not lie, cheat or deceive. Mistrust, once there, is like an axe to the tree of relationship. It is said that 'Trust is like the soul, once gone, is gone forever.'

Integrity, in the sense of plain speaking and above-the-board dealing, is a key quality for all leaders. Leaders who resort to cunning or crafty methods of manipulating people to their will may gain short-term advantages, but in the long run they forfeit trust. Integrity implies adherence to moral standards – especially truth and goodness – that lie outside oneself.

Integrity will always be tested, not least if money is involved. Don't forget who you are, because you see others as you often see yourself.

Be courteous

Courtesy is graceful politeness: being respectful and considerate in your language and behaviour towards others. Courtesy is more than being civil – the bare minimum of common manners and forbearance from crudeness or unpleasantness. It transcends politeness; a dash of warm regard for the feelings or dignity for others, and courtesy is revealed.

Good manners is the art of making other people feel happy and relaxed when we speak to them, and that helps good communication in business as much as in private matters. Courtesy is a business asset. Courtesy is a habit, and without it life would be a lot less enjoyable.

Be generous

A generous person is someone who gives freely without looking for a return. It is not the amount given that counts but rather the readiness to give. A generous spirit is open-minded and liberal in giving on the one hand, and being magnanimous or willing to forgive on the other. A generous person will be naturally helpful by habit. Often human generosity does look for an equal return – we give in order to receive. However, a truly generous spirit lacks this note of self-concern. It is unselfish or self-effacing, intent on the interests of the other without thought of any form of reward.

You do not have to rich to be generous. If you are open-handed to others with help, giving freely and generously of your time, you can find that you receive more than you give. The law of reciprocity – that giving evokes giving – ensues from that fact.

Look after your people – treat them as individuals

Good leaders only have 24 hours in the day like everyone else. 'If only I had enough time' is a natural feeling which challenges all busy people, and who nowadays is not busy? Yet, we will never have any more time. We have, and we have always had, all the time there is. Time is your scarcest resource. It is irreplaceable and irreversible. Few things are more important to a strategic leader than learning how to save time and how to spend it wisely. Time spent on strategic leadership within an organisation is time used wisely. When you become a strategic manager you move out of the boiler room and on to the bridge. A large amount of your time will be spent 'outside the egg' of the company. This may entail travelling to meet major customers, discussions with major allies or being away in connection with major changes to the organisation's structure. You will also be outside the day-to-day running of the business, keeping up to speed on what's going on in your own field or investing time in growing in stature as a strategic leader.

How balanced is your leadership style?

You are employed to achieve the task, build the team and develop the individuals within the team.

1. *Achieving the task* – this involves strategic thinking, planning and implementation, and, most importantly, making it happen.

2. *Building the team* – this involves encouraging teamwork within the team members, based on a balance between a whole team and parts of the team.

3. *Developing the individual* – helping individuals to grow and make their maximum contribution, which helps the individual, team and company.

Principles of time management

Here are some key principles to help you focus on the need to develop the individuals within your team:

1. *Develop a personal sense of time.* You cannot afford to waste your own time or allow others to waste it, wittingly or unwittingly. You've heard of 'value for money' – get 'value for time.'

2. *Identify long-term goals.* Have a vision. State four or five open-ended aims and a set of defining values. You need a guiding principle to help you spend your time wisely.

3. *Make middle-term plans.* You must establish middle-term goals and objectives. These should be specific, time-bound, realistic, stretching and exciting. They must be concrete destinations, likes towns and cities, that the chief parts of the company need to achieve on the road forward to the long-term goals that you have already identified.

On a personal level, you should plan with your team members where they should be aiming their careers so that it gives them a clear path to follow.

4. *Plan the day*. An excellent personal assistant is essential to any strategic leader. Reviewing the week ahead together makes sense at any level of time management. Like any plan, flexibility is essential. If you have to make changes, remember that it is important you make sure those affected know the reasons for doing so.

5. *Make the best use of your best time*. Reserve high-quality time, usually in the morning, for thinking. Solitude and thinking are linked, but you will have plenty of solitude while travelling, or at odd times of the day, such as the lunch-hour, at home at weekends, gardening or driving. Thinking time in strategic leadership involves others, either in a small group or individuals. Some subjects require creativity, wisdom or imagination, so should not be left as an after-thought at the end of a gruelling 10-hour day, or just before you are leaving to catch a train or plane.

6. *Organise office work*. You need support staff who can handle your affairs, and a room where you can work quietly on your own and hold meetings with small groups (round table best) or individuals (comfortable chairs and a coffee table). The less time you spend in your office, the better. When asked why he was so rarely behind a desk, the President of Toyota replied, 'We do not make cars in my office.' As a general rule, if you have asked one of your team to comment on a challenge or issue, always ask them to make recommendations. In other words, get them to bring solutions rather than problems.

7. *Delegate effectively*. This is the golden rule of time management for strategic leaders. Let others be responsible for the day-to-day operation of the business.

In many cases, they are better than you at doing it, so let them get on with it. If they are not, then train them to be! This frees you up for what you are paid for – strategic leadership. Yet delegation should never generate into abdication, the vice of mentally slothful senior managers. You should have a passion for good administration and really value those who deliver it. If you see delegation as a means of developing your people, offer them some demanding and challenging tasks – things you really like to do yourself if time allows.

8. *Remember* – look after the minutes and the hours will look after themselves.

The Japanese way

The best Japanese companies have worked well because they establish a broad direction for their businesses. Bob Tricker (author and economist) has written extensively on Japanese business methods, and here are some of his key principles.

Have a vision

Top management creates the broad, long-term vision for the enterprise as a whole. This is not strategic planning in the sense that it is known and practised in the West. In major Japanese firms, the business leaders share a view of the development of their sectors, and have a vision of their company's place in it, often well into the following decades. This perspective on strategy emphasises corporate values – what the leaders believe is important. It may be captured in a simple, mind-focusing sense of mission – as in NEC's strategic decision to be in the business of 'computers and communications', recognising the convergence of these sectors long before it had become conventional wisdom, or Fujitsu's corporate mission to 'catch IBM' or Komatsu's to 'encircle Caterpillar.' In this way a sense of purpose and commitment is created for everyone in the organisation.

Involve the team

Medium-term plans are created for each business, sector by sector, typically with a three- to five-year focus, complete with competitive, technological and socio-political analysis, and their strategic implications. The process tends to be informal, involving much sharing of information, rather than a formal planning exercise.

Even in the one-year performance budgets, which are the responsibility of middle rather than senior management, the focus seems to be on operational issues, such as requirements for people and funds, rather than on detailed financial analysis. The emphasis is on obtaining commitment to the results rather than creating a basis for control.

The thoughts of Kounosuke Matsushita

A sound leadership approach and vision in terms of broad direction and values was the chief article in Kounosuke Matsushita's (a prominent thinker on social and philosophical questions, as well as a successful industrialist in the 1920s and 1930s) philosophy of management. Manpower, technology, funding, plant and equipment are important to management, but it is even more important, Matsushita believed, that the chief executive should set up sound company goals and ideas and make sure that all his or her employees are thoroughly acquainted and in agreement with them. Such a philosophy is the foundation on which all other elements can be made to work.

Collective wisdom

The key to Japanese success is 'management by collective wisdom.' Matsushita and his contemporaries in firms like Sony, Toyota and Mitsubishi held that no matter how good the manager is, his or her knowledge and abilities are limited. Every employee actively involved in management, freely giving of his or her ideas and innovations, is an indispensable component in the corporate process. To that end of involving the hearts and minds of all to achieve the corporate vision, most Japanese companies have either a *shaze* or a *shakun* – or both.

What are we here for?

Sha means company, *ze* means what is right or justified, *kun* means precept. Thus, *shaze* is a tersely expressed statement, in lofty, high-sounding, formalized language, of corporate ideals and principles, whereas *shakun* is in the same form but directed at a company employee, and tends to be used in ordinary language.

Inspire the team

The original *shaze* or *shakun* is usually written in brush calligraphy, framed and hung in the President's office or the boardroom. In some Japanese companies, it is still customary to recite in unison the *shaze* or *shakun* every morning before starting work, as part of the *chorei* – the inspirational briefing which often begins the week or even the working day. It may last only a few minutes but it helps to create a 'let's go' state of mind and a feeling of identity within the team.

Leadership – a case study

On 13 August 1942, General Bernard Montgomery arrived to take command of the Eighth Army, two months before the Battle of El Alamein. 'The atmosphere was dismal and dreary', he wrote in his diary. That evening he addressed the entire staff of Eighth Army Headquarters, between 50 and 60 officers. As he was their fourth Army Commander within a year, he faced a sceptical audience. The seasoned commanders and staff officers plainly doubted that this new general from Britain was the man to reverse their recent defeats and failures. Montgomery knew that he had to win their minds and hearts that evening if the morale of the broken army was to be restored to full pitch.

He stood on the steps of his predecessor's caravan and addressed the gathering seated on the sand. He spoke without notes, looking straight at the audience. Here is what he said:

> I want first of all to introduce myself to you. You do not know me. I do not know you. But we have got to work together; therefore, we must understand each other and we must have confidence in one another. I have only been here a few hours. But from what I have seen and heard since I arrived, I am prepared to say here and now that I have confidence in you. We will work together as a team; and together we will gain confidence of this great army and go forward to final victory in North Africa.

I believe that one of the first duties of a commander is to create what I call 'atmosphere'; and in that atmosphere, his staff, subordinate commanders and troops will live and work and fight.

I do not like the general atmosphere I find here. It is an atmosphere of doubt, of looking back to select the next place to which to withdraw, of loss of confidence in our ability to defeat Rommel, of desperate defence measures by reserves in preparing positions in Cairo and the Delta. All that must cease. Let us have a new atmosphere ... We will stand and fight here. If we can't stay alive, let us stay dead.

I want to impress on everyone that the bad times are over. Fresh divisions from the UK are now arriving in Egypt, together with ample reinforcements for our present divisions. We have 300 to 400 new Sherman tanks coming and these are actually being unloaded at Suez now. Our mandate from the Prime Minister is to destroy the Axis forces in North Africa; I have seen it written on half a sheet of notepaper. And it will be done. If anyone here thinks it can't be done, let him go at once; I don't want any doubters in this party. It can be done, and it will be done – beyond any possibility of doubt.

What I have done is to get over to you the atmosphere in which we will now work and fight; you must see that, that atmosphere permeates right down through the Eighth Army to the most junior private soldier. All the soldiers must know what is wanted; when they see it coming to pass there will be a surge of confidence throughout the army.

I ask you to give me your confidence and have faith that what I have said will come to pass.

There is much work to be done. The orders I have given about no further withdrawal will mean a complete change in the layout of our dispositions; also that we must begin to prepare for our great offensive ...

'The great point to remember', Montgomery concluded at the famous initial briefing, 'is that we are going to finish with this chap Rommel once and for all. It will be quite easy. There is no doubt about it. He is definitely a nuisance. Therefore we will hit him a crack and finish with him.'

As Montgomery stepped down, the officers rose and stood to attention. 'One could hear a pin drop if such a thing is possible in the sand of the desert', recollected Montgomery. 'But it certainly had a profound effect, and a spirit of hope, anyway with clarity, was born that evening.' His Chief-of-Staff agreed: 'It was one of his greatest efforts', he wrote. 'The effect of the address was electric – it was terrific! And we all went to bed that night with new hope in our hearts, and a great confidence in the future of our Army. I wish someone had taken it down in shorthand, for it would have become a classic of its kind.'

Fortunately, it was taken down in shorthand and filed away for many years.

How the top teams behave

As a team leader, how can you improve your methods in improving the teamwork that exists within your business? One proven technique is to form a concept in your mind of what an excellent team looks like. Then, subconsciously allow that concept to guide you in all that you do and say to achieve it. Below are the characteristics that distinguish an excellent team from teams that don't achieve what they would like to.

- *Clear, realistic and challenging objectives.* The team is focused on what has to be done – broken down into stretching but feasible goals, for both team and individual. Everyone knows what is expected of him or her.

- *Shared sense of purpose.* This doesn't mean that the team can recite the mission statement in unison. What purpose means here is energy plus direction. Engineers call this a vector. It should animate and invigorate the whole team. All share a sense of ownership and responsibility for team success.

- *Best use of resources.* A high-performance team means that resources are allocated for strategic reasons for the good of the whole. They are not seen as the private property of any part of the business. Resources include people and their time, not just money and material.

- *Progress review.* The willingness to monitor its own progress and to generate improvements characterises excellent teams. These improvements encompass process – how we work together – as well as tasks – what we do together.

- *Building on experience.* A blame culture mars any team. Errors will be made, but the biggest mistake of all is to do nothing as to avoid making any! A wise team learns from failure, realising that success teaches us nothing and continual success may breed arrogance.

- *Mutual trust and support.* A good team trusts its members to pursue their part in the common task. Appreciation is expressed and recognition given. People play to each other's strengths and cover each other's weaknesses. The level of mutual support is high. The atmosphere is one of openness and trust.

- *Communication*. People listen to one another and build on one another's contributions. They communicate openly, freely and with skill (clearly, concisely, simply and with tact); issues, problems and weaknesses are not sidestepped. Differences of opinion are respected. Team members know when to be supportive and sensitive, and when to challenge and be intellectually tough.

- *Surfing the waves*. In times of turbulent change, it is never going to be all plain sailing. When unavoidable crises arise, an excellent team rises to the challenge and demonstrates its sterling worth. It has resilience.

When the characteristics above are present within your team, people truly enjoy working together. They have fun, as in other teams, but so rare is the experience of working in an excellent team that the enjoyment and fun are transformed by hindsight into true job satisfaction and a sense of shared gratitude.

> How do you know that you are winning? When the energy is coming the other way and when your people are visibly growing individually and as a group. (Sir John Harvey-Jones)

Building a top team

Fighting elephants

Teamwork at the top – individuals working together towards a common goal – gives an organisation an enormous strength. Businesses that lack teamwork show some basic symptoms of intrigue, politicking and backbiting. Much of the energy is turned inwards towards internal feuds, clashes

157

of ego and trying to outdo each other. The knock-on effect in the business can always be felt. As one African proverb goes, 'When the elephants fight, the grass gets trampled down.' My interpretation of this is that it isn't easy to cut the grass when there are elephants fighting on it. It is sometimes hard enough just cutting the grass, especially if there is a lot of grass and you haven't got a very powerful lawn-mower.

Your role

Are you solely responsible for the business or do you share the responsibility with a partner or colleague? There are a number of advantages and disadvantages for having only one person leading the team. Sir John Harvey-Jones thinks that there are real advantages of having the top job split between two people. It is easier to replace either one of them if some disaster occurs, or if one or the other goes 'off the boil'. The big drawback of having two people at the top is there is often a lack of clarity as to who is ultimately in charge, and where the buck actually stops.

Choosing the top team players

A common weakness of strategic leaders is a lack of judgement about people. It is a bit like driving a car: we all think we are good at it, but how many of us really are? Believing that we can spot 'winners' is as difficult sometimes as it is at a horse race. For the most senior appointments, you should always be on the selection interview. There is a price to pay in getting judgements of people wrong. If someone is not up to the mark and you have to find a replacement, think of the extra time and cost involved, so it is best to get it right first time. Here are a number of team-building tips when choosing your people:

- Avoid selecting clones of yourself. You are looking for a balanced team, with complementary mental gifts of intelligence and imagination, technical and professional experience, and interests relevant to your field.

- Always choose a person of real ability and stature, not those who are guaranteed to accept the party line, agree with what you say and never challenge you in debate before decisions are made. If you appoint 'safe' people who will do your bidding without a word, you are only advertising your own weakness and insecurity.

- You are taking on the whole person, and great strengths are usually accompanied by great weaknesses. A wise and mature team can accommodate far more idiosyncrasies in the best people – providing they are the best – as opposed to being weak characters.

- Never write off a new team member immediately. A person of ability may have been placed – by you or your predecessor – in the wrong role. Reassigned to another, that person may grow wings and fly.

- The opinion of the team on a prospective new member is always worth seeking. But remember that new appointments are ways of changing and improving the team, lifting it out of its comfort zone. Don't expect the team to see gold when you present them with someone who looks like an unrefined piece of ore.

Challenges to teamwork

With all individual team members, there is always a balance between their actual or potential contribution to the task and their eccentricity – some characteristic, action, practice or habit that differs in some way from what is usual or expected.

A mature team will live with idiosyncrasy and reasonable eccentricity, providing talent is there. However, in all teams, there are 'team maintenance' issues, e.g. 'A' does not get on with 'B'. Under normal circumstances all is well, but if things go badly, 'A' will blame 'B' and vice versa. It is the leader's responsibility to help the individuals within the team to bond and work effectively together. This can be achieved by ensuring that the management team themselves are working well together. It is impossible to act as an enabling mechanism if there are unresolved fundamental differences between key management members who share the responsibility for the direction of the company/business.

Building trust within the team

Behaviour is perhaps the most difficult aspect of competence to define and manage. Behaviour is very evident and separate from skills and knowledge. Without the right behaviour, all the skills and knowledge in the world will not help.

> It's your attitude, not your aptitude that determines your altitude. (Anon.)

Leadership is required to ensure that the company's culture and working environment is conducive to producing the team mentality that leads to co-operation, harmony and efficiency. Leadership means taking the lead. This is an area of change that management must move first and not expect an immediate reciprocal step from the people affected by the change. Building trust takes time and demands constancy of purpose.

A number of actions are essential for success.

- Be crystal clear about the organisation's purpose and the core competencies needed to deliver that. Be able to explain these to a cynical workforce. Be clear about the reasons for the change, the benefits for the affected groups and possible pitfalls. Above all be honest.

- Establish, with representatives of the groups involved in the change, the principles upon which a flexible approach to employment is to be built.

- Start with a pilot. Choose a group in which there is some support for such a shift. Do everything possible to make it work and use the supporters who develop from it as evangelists.

- Communicate, communicate, communicate, and in the spirit of two ears to each mouth.

- Work co-operatively with government agencies, unions and other companies following a similar path, but above all with the people who will take advantage of the scheme.

- Expect setbacks. Balance urgency with a recognition that 'Rome wasn't built in a day.'

- Be flexible about how the concept is implemented.

Attract the right people

The process of creating an organisation staffed by people with the right skills, knowledge and behaviours begins with recruitment. Whether it is for full-time or part-time employees, dynamic organisations such as Avis Europe and Disney put enormous effort into attracting the right people.

Indeed, it is during the recruitment process that the customer culture is first emphasised.

The recruitment process stresses the importance of service excellence, and the interviews are to test customer empathy.

In her book *The Complete Guide to Customer Service*, Linda Lash, then of Avis, says, 'The foremost question in the interviewer's mind should be, "What will customers think of this person as a representative of the company?".'

Harvard Professor James Heskett suggests that the skills needed by customer-facing staff include flexibility, tolerance for ambiguity, the ability to monitor and change during the service encounter, and empathy with customers.

It is widely believed that the last of these attributes was found to be more important than age, education, sales-related knowledge, sales training or intelligence.

Motivational meetings

Self-motivation

We are a society that loves parties, rallies and celebrations. The same holds true in business. We love to set high goals and celebrate what we hope will become reality, but we've not been willing to make the required commitment to change.

Everybody talks a good game. Most companies give lip service to taking performance up a notch and being the best that they can be. Most pick a theme for their next company meeting: Riding the Waves of Change!, or Dominate the Market!, or Total Customer Satisfaction, or The Power of the Team, etc. In planning the meeting, they do everything they think they should do. People are sometimes flown to a sunny location or Dublin or head office. The Top People make rousing speeches about vision and mission and celebrating our successes while looking ahead to further heights of greatness. Sometimes there are group sessions and everyone will work in teams and learn about new products and systems. Sometimes there will be a company awards dinner and dinner-dance. If the event is over a number of days, then the session ends with a motivational speaker giving a barn-storming speech and everyone standing up and applauding to music coming from the sound system, with Tina Turner singing 'Simply the Best' at high volume. Sometimes they join hands and sway in unison to the sounds of Queen's 'We are the Champions', and then everyone goes home.

Back at work, management and staff cover their walls with attitude-boosting posters featuring glorious colour photographs of eagles soaring above the clouds, snow-topped mountain summits, and teams (in which there are no 'I's) crossing the finishing line in sweat-drenched celebrations of victory, and dreams come true. In their homes, some tape personal success affirmations to the bathroom mirror and read them every morning before they listen to motivational tapes in the car on the way to work. Surely they are doing everything necessary to scale the summits of success?

What happened?

Months later, people stare into their affirmation-covered bathroom mirrors and some companies look at disappointing figures and they wonder what went wrong. The goal of truly taking performance to a new level wasn't reached. The eagle didn't soar to the mountain top. Perhaps their competition turned out to be simply the best and they are still second. And what's often most deeply frustrating in these situations is that the failure to achieve these goals happens to companies who seemingly have everything going for them, including great people, sound business strategies and excellent products.

So what happened? With all the best-laid plans and all the spine-tingling motivational cheerleading, they never took the critically important first step. They never decided to go. Not really. They just talked about going.

Answer the tough questions

The hard stuff is reaching deep inside and looking honestly into your soul and asking, 'Do we really want to do this and are we willing to change how we've done it up to now?' There are very serious ramifications involved if the answer is 'Yes, we're serious.' The reality may be that you and your company just may not be willing to do what it takes to achieve greatness. Which is fine. Just be clear on what you are committing to if you say, 'We mean it. Let's go.' It's much better not to kid yourselves and freely choose to stay where you are. The reality might be that you have spent years as a company fighting your way to the middle of the pack and now you just want to rest for a while. No problem. Of course, the inherent danger in that strategy is that there's really no such thing as a holding position. You're either gaining ground or losing ground.

It is better to be honestly average and try to stay where you are with a sense of contentment than be unrealistically ambitious about what is yet to be and never get there because you never really wanted to go there in the first place. It is demoralising to any group of people to say year after year that this is the year that we go to the mountain top, when all that ever happens is we just keep doing what we've been doing with a new set of posters on the wall.

Believe then become

Quill is a leading direct marketer of office supplies in the USA. At Quill they painted a picture of what success would look like for everyone and then began putting the pieces in place. They developed a new and simplified vision statement and then drove home the fact that leadership was the way they were going to bring themselves to the level they wanted. They developed the Quill Leadership Model and then taught leadership throughout the company. Many things were done for effect – for example, putting their logo on everything in order to promote team spirit. Everybody at Quill was focused on one strategic principle, 'We take better care of our customers than anyone else.' To drive home the message, the Quill Leadership Institute was created. As a result Quill people believe that they are the best, they know where they need to go and they are developing the tools to get there.

Challenge your people

One of my delegates came into a course that I was running and said that he couldn't motivate his staff. He said that he had tried to coax them, push them, promised them rewards, had threatened them, even sworn at them. But nothing had worked. He said, 'They just don't produce.' Another delegate had remarked that he had tried a novel idea. He said that they produced a number of products in a shift. These were measured in pallets. He put up a blackboard in the staff room and chalked up a number 5 on the board. The next morning, the night shift had rubbed out the 5 and replaced it with a 6. When the day shift reported for work, they saw the 6 chalked on the board. The reaction was competition between the two shifts to pitch in more effort and enthusiasm, and before long the factory, which had lagged behind in production compared with others in the group, was turning out more work than any other. The principle? As my delegate friend said to me, 'The way to get things done is to stimulate competition. Not just in a money-sense but in the real desire to excel.'

'The desire to excel! the challenge! A sure fire way of appealing to people of spirit.'

Harvey Firestone, who founded the Firestone Tire and Rubber Company, was quoted as saying, 'Pay and pay alone will never bring together or hold good people. I think it is the game itself.' Frederick Herzberg, a management scientist who wrote about what motivates and de-motivates people, studied thousands of people, ranging from factory workers to senior executives. What do you think he found to be the most motivating part of their jobs? Money? Good working conditions? Fringe benefits? None of the above. The major factor that motivated people was the work itself. If the work was exciting and interesting, the worker looked forward to doing it and was motivated to do a good job.

This is what every successful person loves: 'the game.' It gives the chance for self-expression, the chance to prove his or her worth, to excel, to win. This is what makes competing in a swimming gala, a fun-run or ten-pin bowling fun: the desire to excel, the desire for a feeling of importance and achievement.

Working together, succeeding together

Klaus Kobjoll owns the Schindlerhof Hotel in Nuremberg, Germany. The hotel's main aim is to make everyone's visit an unforgettable experience. Enjoyment, harmony and freedom are the values on which the hotel builds its corporate vision and overall beliefs.

One of the key factors that bring success to the Schindlerhof is the success of the hotel's employees. Everyone can control their own success by the degree to which they identify with the belief that warm-heartedness and amiability are their top priorities. So what are Klaus Kobjoll's main reasons for running such a successful hotel. He has lots of ideas that we can borrow.

Money, money, money

There's practically nothing in the world that can't be made less well and sold for less money, and people who only go by price are the well-deserved prey of such dealings. It is unwise to pay too much, but it is worse not to pay enough. When you pay too much, you lose money – that is all. However, when you don't pay enough, you sometimes lose everything, as the object you buy cannot meet the requirements expected of it.

The law of economy makes it impossible to get good value for a small amount of money. If you accept the lowest offer, you must allow something for the risk you are taking. And if you do that, then you have enough money to pay for something better.

All employees are TUNED into customer care

Klaus believes that employees have to play a TUNE to enable total customer satisfaction.

- T – *Touched with the Schindlerhof spirit*. Klaus and Renate Kobjoll believe that you have to have a personal vision of sense and meaning. Their values for the team include no hierarchical behaviour, no privileges, everyone encouraged to make decisions and an acceptance of responsibility, pleasure in learning from mistakes, and a friendly working atmosphere.

- *U – Use of all the quality standards.* All employees are encouraged to deliver consistent quality standards. This is achieved by encouraging all team members to learn both on and off job. All team members are encouraged to take full responsibility for their own learning, and quality manuals are introduced from Day 1. These are emphasised throughout every team member's time at the Schindlerhof.

- *N – Natural well-being.* Making the right impression with your customers (internal and external) can act as SOFTEN relationships. S – smile, O – open posture, F – forward lean, T – touch, E – eye contact, N – nod. Kobjoll says that if you are too concerned with yourself, you can't give enough attention to the person you are supposed to be communicating with. He also advises that details are decisive. You can never spend enough time on them. And we never know which details concern each individual customer.

- *E – Energy. Energia* (Greek for energy) means effectiveness. Energy can be transmitted, it is infectious and creates enthusiasm among staff and customers. This can be achieved by: anticipating and sensing guests' wishes, keeping to schedules and keeping promises, steering a steady course even under severe pressure (especially when dealing with non-standard customer requests), making sure that details are well thought through so that the customer always views the service as positive.

Team evaluations

Klaus has developed an innovative staff performance model that measures everyone's value to themselves and to the business. He calls this PIX – Player Index. Each team member earns points by giving ideas, helping in hotel projects (in their own time), by length of service, punctuality, personal job evaluation, training days attended, fitness (body mass index), etc. Points are deducted for days lost through illness, breach of game rules, smoker/non-smoker, mistake quota, etc.

> Positive thinking works like an immune system against failure! To lead a company means to learn how to 'let go!' (Klaus Kobjoll)

Setting goals

> When I want to, I perform better than when I have to. I want to for me, I have to for you. (Anon.)

Self-motivation is a matter of choice.

It is always good to give yourself something to aim towards. It is also useful to have performance goals.

1. *An end goal* is a final objective – to become the market leader, to be appointed sales director, to land a certain key account, to win a gold medal. It is not always within your absolute control as you cannot know or control what your competitors will do.

2. *A performance goal* is when you identify the performance level that you believe will provide you with a very good chance of achieving the end goal. It is largely within your

control and it generally provides a means of measuring progress – 99% of production to pass quality control first time, for us to sell 2,000 widgets this month, to run a mile in under six minutes by the end of September, etc. It is far easier to take responsibility for a performance goal that is within your control, than an end goal, which is not. An end goal whenever possible should be supported by a performance goal. The end goal may provide the inspiration, but the performance goal defines the specification.

Whose goal?

The value of choice and responsibility in terms of self-motivation should never be underestimated, e.g. if a sales team comes up with a goal that is lower than the boss wishes, he or she should consider the consequences very carefully before overriding their figure and imposing one of his or he own. The boss may do better to swallow his or her pride and accept their figure. Insisting on his or her figure may well have the effect of lowering the performance of the team even though the boss's target was higher than theirs. They may or may not consider his or her figure discouragingly unrealistic, but they will certainly be de-motivated by their lack of choice. The boss also has the option to start with the team's figure and coach them upwards by exploring and helping them to dismantle their barriers to achieving more. They then retain responsibility for the finally agreed figure.

Qualities of a good goal

In addition to supporting an end goal, which is not within your control, with a performance goal, which is, goals need to be not only SMART:

- specific
- measurable
- agreed
- realistic
- time-bound

but PURE:

- positively stated
- understood
- relevant
- ethical

and CLEAR:

- challenging
- legal
- environmentally sound
- appropriate
- recorded

If the goal is not *realistic*, there is no hope, but if it is not *challenging*, there is no motivation. So there is a middle ground into which goals should fit.

A sample coaching session

1. Douglas (coachee) – 'I want to lose weight and be a lot fitter too.'

2. Mary (coach) – 'So Douglas what weight do you want to get down to?'

3. Douglas – 'About 14 stones by the end of the summer, so lose 20 pounds.'

4. Mary – '14 stones by what date exactly?'

5. Douglas – '25th of September.'

6. Mary – 'Today is April 20th, so that gives us five months, so that means an average of four pounds a month. How much do you want to lose by July 1st?'

7. Douglas – '10 pounds by then.'

8. Mary – 'You could do that by not eating and yet not be that much fitter. How can we measure fitness?'

9. Douglas – I'll start running 20 miles a week from next Monday.'

10. Mary – 'At what speed?'

11. Douglas – 'I'll be happy just to run 20 miles a week.'

12. Mary – 'It doesn't matter about how fast you go, just give yourself a target speed. What will it be?'

13. Douglas – 'OK, nine-minute miles.'

Douglas now has a goal, a long-term goal and a half-way goal. His goals are specific, measurable and probably incorporate all the qualities recommended. Because there are no corporate imperatives in Douglas's case, he has complete and total control of his own goals.

Performance and development reviews

These interviews should be conducted off-the-job; the whole process involves team members in thinking about their work as they perform it, learning and improving on the job, before and after the interview. It is linked with a team member's personal development plan. The interview can be seen as a coaching session, providing an opportunity to discuss the work situation and to seek to improve what the team member is doing. It is possible to operate an entire performance development and review system on a competence basis. Some companies have competence-based performance management systems, which means development tends to be competence-based too. The old term 'appraisal' is less referred to nowadays, because it accents the judgmental rather the developmental. HR managers have had to find other terminology to support such initiatives.

360-degree feedback

Increasingly, performance reviews are not seen just as a one-to-one exchange between employee/manager and his or her manager, but as a question for a broader audience within the company (and occasionally beyond it). The review process is 360° feedback when it extends to include an employee's peers and people who work directly below them, perhaps other colleagues whose roles impinge on the subject's, and in some cases contacts from external organisations, notably customers, but also suppliers or other business partners.

The origins of terms are sometimes explained like this: 90° appraisal review refers to a traditional, downward appraisal; 180° appraisal adds upward feedback; 270° appraisal includes views of team members and colleagues; 360° adds all individual 'appraisees' and their managers; and finally 450° appraisal adds in customers and suppliers. It should be noted that the 360° feedback conveys a sense of consulting the full circle of concerned parties.

The technique of 360° feedback has been criticised for generating too much paperwork, and this becoming a bureaucratic process. However, web-enabled technology is easing these problems, both by reducing unnecessary paper and by speeding things up, especially with large numbers of participants spread over a wide area.

Case study – Philips Electronics

Amsterdam-based Koninklijke Philips Electronics NV is a global giant, with 200 production sites in over 25 countries, and sales and service outlets in 150 countries, employing 200,000 people worldwide. The brand name, Philips, is known to many markets, from lighting to consumer electronic goods, semiconductors and medical systems. Philips recognises the vital significance of developing its managers to help sustain its competitiveness and to spearhead its drive to attain world-class excellence.

The company operates a career development programme, which embraces a range of activities such as work simulation exercises, psychometric assessments and coaching. A key component of the programme is 360° feedback, which is used exclusively for development and not assessment purposes, to encourage a frank and open climate.

Rather than use an off-the-shelf feedback package, Philips have commissioned their own bespoke version, which is based on their in-company leadership competences. The documentation is easy and simple to complete, fits the corporate culture and utilises information technology, with e-mail distribution and computer-scanned answer sheets.

The outputs include a personalised, confidential report for each participant, featuring ideas and activities to address his or her highlighted development needs. The participants have access to self-development materials, and managers have access to a leadership development pack, which provides more general ideas and guidance.

The system ensures a clear, public development platform for managers to see for themselves how they compare to the world-class standard required and what they have to do to achieve career progression.

You get what you reward!

This is one of the greatest management principles used today in the business world. Below is an example to explain the principle:

You have two employees A and B. A is incredibly talented and B is a marginal performer. You give similar assignments to both. A completes his or her task before it is due and returns it with no errors. Because A is finished you give him or her additional assignments as a matter of fact. Meanwhile B is not only late with their assignment but when he or she finally turns in their work, it is full of errors. Because you are now under severe time restrictions, you accept B's work and then amend/correct it yourself. This is something you should *never* do!

The question then is, 'who is actually being rewarded?'

The answer is B of course – he or she has learned that submitting work that is substandard and late is OK and that you as his or her manager will fix it.

That is clearly a case of rewarding an employee who doesn't deserve one; and A is being punishing for being a diligent, outstanding worker. A will soon realise that by doing their best is not in his or her best interest and soon will become a B or will B off!

Hence the world famous slogan, 'You get what you reward (deserve)!'

Important points in human relations

This short section is about dealing with difficult people, not difficult situations. It's about focusing on the people. By understanding people, how they tick, what they think and why they act the way they do, we can avoid the bad times and horrible situations, and overcome the awkward issues.

Use the following phrases more in everyday language and you will notice that you will deal with and influence people more easily:

- The six most important words: 'I admit, I made a mistake.'

- The five most important words: 'You did a good job.'

- The four most important words: 'What is your opinion?'

- The three most important words: 'Would you mind?'

- The two most important words: 'Thank you.'

- The most important word: 'We'.

- The least important word: 'I'.

If you plant some seeds and the flowers don't grow, it's no good blaming the flower. It may be the soil, the fertiliser, a lack of water, etc. We just have to find out what the problem is and fix it. If we are having difficulties with families, the people we work with or our friends, what's the point of blaming them? Figure out the reason and then fix it.

Difficult, who me?

Yes, you! Before you can think about dealing with difficult people, let's start with you. Are you difficult? Are you the one out of step? Are you the one with the problem? Here is some bad news for you: nice people are not always like you!

I know that the world would be a much simpler place if everyone was like you, but they're not. They will have different backgrounds, different educations, different perspectives and different ambitions. They will be motivated differently and think differently. And they can still be nice people!

Really difficult people are most likely to be selfish and inwardly focused. They won't really care about you. For them, it's all about them. So don't let them get under your skin. When dealing with people – *Don't take it personally!*

Ask yourself, 'What do I want to get out of this encounter?' Decide in advance:

- what is the purpose of this encounter?;
- what are the key results you want to achieve?;
- do you have to change your behaviour to get the most out of the encounter?

If someone is being rude to you, try this strategy: 'I'm not sure what you meant by that remark. Can you explain it to me please?' It normally leads to the other person toning down their language.

This may come as something as a shock, but there aren't too many people out there who care too much about you. There's your mother, she probably loves you, your family, partners and a few friends too. However, when push comes to shove, you're on your own. How we treat each other is largely a product of how we feel about each other. Most people started off neutral, some downright antagonistic but most couldn't care less about you.

As for difficult people – they don't care about you at all! They care about themselves. That's why they're difficult. What can you do about them? Well not much! It is unlikely that we are going to change them. So why bother? There is a much easier way – remember that difficult people are predictable people.

How many times have you heard people say, 'Oh, don't bother with him, he's a misery.' Or 'Don't ask her, she finds fault in everything.' You see difficult people are not just difficult with you. They are concerned with themselves and are usually difficult with everyone. Predictable situations are relatively easy to deal with. You can prepare in advance how to deal with difficult people. They are stuck in their ways. All you have to do is move around them. It may mean using your brain rather than your emotions. Decide what you want in advance and go for it.

- If you are dealing with a nit-picker and a stickler for detail, give them detail. 'In the report, I've included all the background I can think of, including spreadsheets for three different examples. Let me know if there's anything else you need.'
- If someone is abrupt, get straight to the point, avoid flannel and go to the heart of the matter.
- If someone is an egomaniac, tell them how good they are.

The strategy is straight-forward. You will not change a difficult person by being difficult. Remember, they don't care about you, they care about themselves. By deciding in advance what you want out of the encounter and being prepared to sidestep and change your approach, you can achieve what you want.

Looking after the team

The workplace in 2005 is a very different environment for many businesses from ten or twenty years ago. Companies realise that they must look after their team members and make their working areas and company culture as comfortable and stress-free as possible.

Employees are often seen rushing around the shops at lunchtime, dashing to the supermarket on the way home in the evening and fixing the car at the weekend. At Merck's New Jersey campus, staff can leave the car for an oil change, drop off dry cleaning and shoe repairs, ask the travel service to book a holiday and arrange for a wrapped gift to be sent. On the way out of the building, employees can pick up a movie and a freshly prepared evening meal. Merck – dubbed 'Mother Merck' by the *New York Times* – is not alone. Texas Instruments' concierges will fix your car. Sun Microsystems will do your dry-cleaning.

A helping hand

In Britain, Accenture has a concierge service. Corporate concierges will book tickets, send flowers, advise on theatre options and receive personal deliveries. Lehman Brothers, an investment bank, has established an internal concierge system to deal with personal requests. 'We are competing for the brightest and the best' says Karl Dannebaum, Managing Director. 'This is a way of getting and keeping them.'

Once the shopping is taken care of, you might feel like a haircut. No problem. MBNA International Bank has a hairdresser on site. Netscape has a dentist on site. Companies are also offering a range of therapies. Advertising company HHCL has a massage and acupuncture room.

Medical services

Medical services are increasingly available in the workplace. A growing number of on-site centres offer standard medical testing and advice. Larger firms in the USA offer cancer screening, blood tests and X-rays. Work, once a survival course in physically arduous conditions, has gone considerably softer, tending carefully to physical, mental and emotional needs.

Someone to listen

Employee counselling is one of the fastest-growing services in the UK. Knowledge work, after all, is mind work, so companies worry as much about mental as physical health. Originally intended to help workers with work-related problems, most counselling is now general, tackling any problem that is affecting an employee's mental well-being.

An employee working for a television production company who had gone to the company's counsellor when a failed relationship had knocked her sideways said:

> The first time I saw the counsellor I just sat and cried. I dread to think what would have happened if the counselling had not been available. I think I would have left the company. I could have been on Prozac. At least half our department has been to see her. (*The Scotsman*, 17 April 2000)

Scottish Amicable has a contract with the Employee Counselling Service. The director of the service, Pauline Bryan, says it pays for itself by freeing up management time that would otherwise be used dealing with the consequences of mental health problems. Managers can end up spending hours trying to help people with what are not really work-related issues.

Working up a sweat

As long ago as the 1920s, E. K. Hall of American Telephone and Telegraph said, 'We must find ways to help our workers get their worries out of their minds so that they can get on with the job and be "up for it".'

A sure way to be 'up for it' as well as laying the foundation of good mental health is to take regular exercise. So it is no surprise that some companies are in this game too, encouraging staff not only to work out their problems but work out their bodies. At 3.00 p.m. at Electronic Arts, half a dozen staff are building up a sweat, swapping keyboards for bench presses in the gym. The firm has a running track too. Lots of firms have gyms and fitness centres, or at least have a deal with a nearby gym. We may work in deodorised dryness in air-conditioned offices, but it doesn't mean there's no sweating at work.

How to be an effective coach

IBM and more recently the Post Office carried out research with regard to how people were able to recall training that they had experienced. A group of people were divided randomly into three subgroups, each of which was taught something quite simple, the same thing, using three different approaches. The results below speak for themselves. It shows how dramatically recall declines when people are only told something. This could be worrying if learning 'life-saving' skills for example.

	Told	Told and shown	Told, shown and experienced
Recall after 3 weeks	70%	72%	85%
Recall after 3 months	10%	32%	65%

In responding to coaching questions, the learner becomes aware of every aspect of the task and actions necessary. This clarity enables him or her to envisage the near certainty of success, and so to choose to take responsibility. By listening to the answers to the coaching questions, the coach knows not only the action plan, but also the thinking that went into it. The coach is far better informed than they would be if he or she told the employee what to do, and therefore has better control of what is going on. As the dialogue and the relationships in coaching are non-threatening and supportive, no behaviour change occurs when the manager is absent. Coaching can provide managers with real control and provides the team member with real responsibility.

Your role as a manager

Many managers think that they don't have the time to coach their people and send them on training courses instead. They seldom get their money's worth.

If they spend time coaching their team members, the developed staff shoulder much greater responsibility, freeing the manager from fire-fighting, not only allowing them to coach more but to attend to other issues that only he or she can deal with.

Timing, quality and learning

If time is the predominant criterion in a situation (e.g. in an immediate crisis), doing the job yourself or telling someone exactly what to do will probably be the fastest way. If quality is the key factor, coaching for high awareness and responsibility is likely to be the best way. If maximising learning is predominant (e.g. someone passing their driving test), clearly coaching will optimise learning and its retention.

In most situations in the workplace, time quality and learning all have some relevance all of the time. Time normally takes precedence over quality, and learning is usually relegated to third place. Managers have a hard time giving up telling and in turn business performance in most establishments falls short of what it might be or could be.

If managers adopted the principles of coaching, they could get the job done to a higher standard and develop their people at the same time. It sounds too good to be true, but you could have 250 days of the year getting the job done and at the same time have 250 days of the year of staff development per person, *if* you practise a manager/coach approach back in the workplace.

7

Getting things done

Sources of inspiration

How creative are you?

Creative and innovative people have energy; they practically run to places because they cannot wait to start things. They are animated, excited and may think of many more ideas than they actually have the time to implement. They often work hard and play hard and in the playing often come up with even more innovation. However, not everyone has this energy; some of us have to work at it. So where do you start?

Ideas generation

From the minute that you know you have to generate ideas, to be creative or to design a plan or project, park the broad parameters in your mind. If you have the space, put the title of your project on a large piece of paper or flipchart, and, either using Post-its or felt-tipped pens, add ideas as they occur to you. Make things as visible as possible and keep adding. As the ideas begin to flow, even the most insignificant points may ultimately become an important feature of the end result.

In the early stages, it is important that you do not force the process; if you find ideas are not flowing, leave it and do something else. Often people find that by doing something completely different their minds will start generating ideas. Creative thinking can also take place during sleep. If you focus on the problem before you go to sleep, something called the 'Theta' process takes over and the mind produces its own solutions that are there when you wake. Here are some ideas to help you generate ideas:

- identify the times when you have your best ideas – create the environment that works for you, e.g. perhaps a special place or room or playing music;
- some find that taking part in certain leisure activities helps their creative thinking, e.g. swimming, walking or climbing;
- equip yourself with the right resources, sharp pencils, lots of paper, coloured pens, etc.;
- spend some time researching by talking to friends, reading books, looking up websites, etc.;
- build up your own resources of material, i.e. photographs, press cuttings, articles – if you have an idea write it down even if you aren't going to use it immediately (you can use it in the future);
- build up a network of contacts, colleagues, friends, managers, mentors, people you know who are a source of good ideas.

Running an ideas-generating session

There are a number of techniques that you can use to foster the generation of ideas. Everyone will develop their preferred way of operating, and those listed below have been used successfully by many individuals and organisations.

Brainstorming

This is one of the simplest techniques for working with groups. This is facilitated by using a flipchart with a single heading and then noting down as many thoughts as possible, randomly, without any attempt to rank or order them. These should be written down as single words or short phrases. The technique is designed to help with the flow of ideas and there are important rules, e.g. no editing, no qualifying, no restricting. The concept works because one person's thoughts often stimulate others and, by not interrupting each other, ideas can flow very quickly. Analysis takes place later. The activity often also creates an energy and an element of fun within the group.

SWOT (strengths, weaknesses, opportunities, threats)

This is a way of adding structure to a brainstorm. By dividing a piece of flipchart into four and adding headings, strengths, weaknesses, opportunities and threats, a group may analyse their business, the workings of the group, future business potential or any other aspect that seems appropriate. Strengths and weaknesses are often perceived as current and internal issues, and opportunities and threats as future and external issues. Once the areas have been identified, different groups can work on the outcomes, e.g. 'What can we do as a business to minimise the threats we have identified?'

Mind-mapping

This technique was invented by Tony Buzan (Chairman of the Brain Foundation and an author on the subject of mind-mapping and organising information). It comprises a series of thoughts written on paper to help gather a systematic thinking structure when you are note-taking, problem-solving, planning or reviewing. Large amounts of information can be summarised on one page, and from this initial map-project plans can be developed. Certain aspects can be given to particular people for further development, but you always retain a very visual model of the total picture and also the start of the process. For more details e-mail Tony Buzan at *Buzan@mind-map.com*.

Creative problem-solving

This is an effective management tool, and a key rule is to encourage people to think 'outside the box'. The following points should be considered:

- Qualify and clarify the problem; share information.
- Agree processes/problem-solving techniques; explore options.
- Share known information (SWOT); use questions, i.e. when, where, why, what and how.
- Allow gestation periods on all solutions; agree and implement action points.

How to gain inspiration

Leadership is about providing direction and building teamwork. It is also about inspiring your people. But who inspires you? We are all different. What matters is that each of us discovers pots of inspiration that lie along the long road of life. The road goes straight, then bends, goes uphill and down, and we need to find inspiration so that we can 'walk the walk' with our colleagues.

Seize the day

Always be aware of possibilities; seek and search and be enterprising. Here is an example. Professor Terry Hamlin experienced many up and downs while working in various different hospitals. He recalls, 'Some time ago, there was a laundry strike at the hospital that resulted in spare funds. I laid claim to the money and used it to buy a specific piece of equipment needed in my department. The thing was, I could only use the money in £1,000 chunks, so I had the equipment delivered in parts, each with a separate invoice. That piece of equipment has become instrumental in the treatment of bone-marrow disease world-wide.'

Sources of inner conviction

Ordway Tead (an author who has debated the relationship between capitalism and democracy and the balance between workers, managers and owners) wrote in *The Art of Leadership* that a good leader has faith. Faith is sometimes defined as 'the giving substance to things hoped for and as a conviction of things not seen.' Faith brings about an active effort to bring good to pass based on the confirming experience that such activity is and does good. It is not a mere fatuous trust in something nor the mere wish for something. It is a collaboration, which the individual finds through his or her efforts, of his or her sense that worth is being achieved.

Futilitarianism has no place in your thinking

Futilitarianism is the philosophy that all human striving is futile; it is no philosophy for a strategic leader. The leader is essentially the affirmer, the doer and the creator. He or she believes that purposes can be achieved, that experience can be directed and controlled, and that events can moulded to the desired result. No one lavishes energy and creative effort on any project for long unless they believe the task is worth doing.

The experience of great leaders suggests positivity is an important element that leads to success. They have seemed in many instances to discover their faith and power in meeting and overcoming insurmountable obstacles, in refusing to admit defeat, in sacrificing to the limit of their cause. They may have suffered the depths of their being as one of the prices paid for the superb confidence and courage they were gradually able to manifest.

Inspiration is everywhere

The media – television, radio, journals, magazines, newspapers, the internet – may be laden with bad news about human nature, but they also bring to light fantastically inspiring examples. What is extraordinary is how ordinary people reveal a nobility of spirit in adversity that humbles and inspires those around them and sometimes those afar. There are buckets of inspiration in the lives of others, and you only need a few drops each day to help you keep things in perspective, renew your vital interests and stay on purpose.

> It's no good trying to shine if you don't have time to fill your lamp. (Robert Browning)

Identify as many different sources of inspiration (oil) as you can to keep your light shining brightly. There are gallons of hidden reserves, beneath the soil of human nature – enough to last as long as the sun. You will run into deserts on your journey, desolate places where others often abandon hope. Yet there is always a well of inspiration ahead of you if you persevere.

> In the deserts of the heart, let the healing fountain start. (W. H. Auden)

Inspire yourself

Morale – our basic attitude to the task in hand – has to have spiritual foundations if it is to endure all the vicissitudes of life. As a leader in your own life, you need to check those foundations are in place as much as a general does when in command of an army. You are in command of yourself, and so you need to reflect on the same agenda if your own morale is to remain high.

Let TLA help you make changes

TLA (talking–listening–acting) is one of our most powerful functions.

We talk to ourselves, we listen to what we say to ourselves and we act accordingly to what we say. As far as we know, it is exclusively human. Animals listen to and follow their senses and their instincts. Our TLA goes on automatically, often unconsciously and often disastrously. We are nearly always talking; even when we are not talking aloud we are usually talking to ourselves. We are our best audience; we never interrupt. Even when we are asleep, there is some evidence that part of ourselves is still talking, and part is still listening. We are our own captive audience, 24 hours a day.

TLA is also used by others, and we can act on their suggestions. Modern merchandising makes cunning use of this human susceptibility with the immense semi-captive audience of radio and television. By using TLA wisely, we can change external situations, which are almost always involved with our feelings, words and actions, and which can be directly influenced by TLA. We must first recognise the power of TLA – then decide to *use* it instead of being used *by* it.

For example, perhaps you are often tired. There is little sense in telling yourself that you feel fresh and energetic, when it is obviously not true. But if I say 'I am always tired', I am confirming a state that is only likely to be transitory. How much better to use my telling, listening and acting power not to confirm but to alleviate my fatigue. Instead of 'I am always tired', I might say, 'I can rest completely.'

Another example may be someone who says 'I can never remember people's names.' If the person looks more realistically at the situation, and prepares the ground to remember people's names rather than indulging in negative self-talk, then a more positive outcome is far more likely.

Change your attitude

Many of the difficult situations that we face are of our own making, and our negative and destructive TLA. The answer to this challenge is to substitute good-sense talk for nonsense talk. TLA is always with us, ready to work with us or against us. By stopping self-destructive repetition and making a fair appraisal of a situation, one can arrive at a more constructive, more creative way of directing oneself without distorting the truth.

Making changes

Whatever you want to improve, whether it is your health, your ability to get along with people, your memory or your golf stroke, the method should be the same: use your TLA. Try the following technique.

- Make a list of the traits or behaviour patterns you want to change. These changes may include almost anything that is changeable.

- Choose one change at a time. Stay with it until you have achieved it. Then choose another.

- Put your wished for attainment in a phrase. Say only what you know is possible. Say it in the present, not the future tense.

Don't say, 'Beginning from tomorrow, I will stop ...' This will always remain in the future. How many times have you heard someone say, 'I will start tomorrow, next week, next month, etc.' Better to say, 'Here and now, I will ...' This gives you direction *now*. When using TLA, use a simple phrase in the present tense, e.g. 'It is getting better' or 'I am feeling more confident about this now.'

Once you have chosen your phrase:

- Choose a rhythmical tune. Combine that tune in rhythm with the words of your phrase. Sing the phrase aloud if you are alone, silently if you are not.

- Sing the phrase in time with your movements as you perform a muscular exercise, e.g. tightening your stomach muscles, walking, squeezing a ball or any action that can be rhythmically performed.

- Repeat the same phrase while resting and relaxing during the daytime, and – most importantly – repeat it until you go to sleep at night. When resting and relaxing, do not sing the phrase, but repeat it silently until you go to sleep.

■ Sing the phrase the moment you wake up in the morning and while you dress. Sing it as you prepare to go to work, shopping or to an appointment.

This combined approach is very powerful. It is important to speak to ourselves in a clear and constructive way. When your mind tries to go into destructive TLA mode, quickly replace it with your chosen phrase.

In his book *Creative Realism*, Dr Rolf Alexander gives some examples of phrases that can help you develop your own unique phrase, e.g.:

■ It is getting easier to make decisions.

■ It is getting more pleasant to meet new people.

■ Stop talking nonsense now; stop now!; start now!

■ Change is possible.

■ I can change; I can do it!

■ Change (your attitude) now!

This technique will work for you – if you work at it!

Thinking differently

There are a number of techniques that help us to think 'outside the box.'

■ *Synectics*. Originated by William Gordon, synetics means joining unassociated irrelevant elements. It picks up on the idea that analogous thinking is a natural creative activity. Many accounts of how naturally creative people and geniuses go about their work seem to reveal that analogy often comes into it. There are two parts.

- *Make a connection.* When dealing with the problem, make a connection between the unfamiliar and the familiar. This is called making the strange familiar. It is achieved by asking questions such as 'How is a leaf like a snack?' (Answer – if it's a Pringle).

- *Different perspectives.* Look at the problem from a variety of different angles: the search for novel viewpoints. This is called making the familiar strange. Ask questions like: 'How is a chocolate bar like an animal?' (Answer – it's a Lion).

To help elicit ideas you can 'chunk up' and 'chunk down' logical categories by generalising or specifying. So a crisp becomes a snack, becomes a food, becomes a garnish, becomes a decoration, etc.

Attribute zapping

One of the archetypal tests for creativity activities is to find a use for a familiar object. For instance, in the creativity column of the *Independent*, readers were asked just that.

Q. What can you do with an odd sock?

A. Use as a tool to measure right-angles.

A. Set up an emotional reunion with the other sock on TV.

A. Protect cucumbers from the frost.

A. TV show – one foot in the sock.

A. Cushion for a pogo stick.

A. Feed it baked beans and use it for a wind sock.

A. Starch it and use it as a boomerang.

Can you think of any more? Try this simpler one.

Q. How many uses can you find for a brick?

A way to think up ideas of uses is to look at the attributes of the brick and generate ideas from each of them. For example, the brick can be described as: red, rough, cuboid, sharp-edged, heavy, having two holes, etc. To create uses for the brick just take each attribute in turn and ask, 'What can I do with the sharp edges?', 'What can I do with the redness?' and so on.

Chindogu

Chindogu is a transitional idea. It is a Japanese term that comes from the word *chin* meaning 'unusual' and *dogu* meaning 'tool.' It is a gadget that appears to be useful but really isn't. The rules for *chindogu* are that the gadgets must be capable of being made, but must not be useful (just nearly useful). It is gratuitous invention, with the main purpose being *fun*. Here are some rules:

- it must make your life more convenient in some way but inconvenient in another way;
- it can't be for real use;
- it must actually work;
- it has a spirit of anarchy;
- it is a tool for everyday life;
- it is humorous in some way.

For example:

- a Swiss army glove – a glove with a tool on each digit;
- a hay fever dispenser – a toilet roll holder that sits on the head to dispense toilet roll for hay fever sufferers.

These inventions, no matter how crazy they seem, can then be evaluated. Can you see any sense in them? Could they be the spark for any really useful ideas? Because the starting points for *chindogus* are the little irritations of normal life, and they occur in the stimuli of everyday contexts and settings, it would be possible to use real settings, situations or irritations to begin the process.

Other techniques

- *Force field diagrams* – for analysing driving and restraining forces in change situations.
- *Ishikawa (fishbone) diagrams* – for problem-solving.
- *SWOT analysis* – for identifying and evaluating internal factors (strengths and weaknesses) and external factors (opportunities and threats) in organisational contexts.

Not everyone will respond to all of these techniques outlined above, but most will find a few that will suit their own style of working.

Being creative

Creative techniques involve engaging different aspects of our thought processes. Of course, individual differences mean that we use unique combinations of different kinds of thinking methods, but it is also true that different people favour some over others.

The different approaches to creativity involve some combination of our focus on verbal, visual and metaphorical thinking.

Verbal

Many of our thought processes are based around language. There is a close relationship between concepts and language. Therefore, it makes sense for many people to use verbal techniques to provoke and elicit ideas. Give your brain a workout by guessing the well-known phrases or sayings from the clues below:

1. KJUSTK

2. YOUJUSTME

3. GET IT, GET IT, GET IT, GET IT

4. ie.

5. INVA DERS

You have to think quite deeply for the answers to these, don't you? Did you notice that most of your processing occurred under the level of consciousness? The lateral and associative talents of your brain need to be applied, as it is very difficult to arrive at the answers by purely logical, sequential means.

Visual

A picture is worth a thousand words

Most of us live in complex and overloaded information spaces. On a daily basis we can quickly reach the limit of our brain's ability to consciously process and retain information in a useful form. It is not surprising that we need to develop tools and techniques that help us cope with this overload.

There is technology available to enable us to process information once it is organised and externalised. But there is much less help when it comes to the primary information processor available – the brain.

For many people the visual channel is the primary means of dealing with complex, conceptual information. Dealing with large amounts of information, and the relationships between the components of the information, is probably best done visually.

Concept space maps (or microcosms/spider diagrams) are ideal tools for displaying such information. These are a visual arrangement that shows concepts 'in relation to'. They encapsulate large amounts of complex data in a 'mind's eye chunk' They mirror the natural associative and relational patterns of the brain. Using the power of the visual imagination, microcosm diagrams will help you visualise concepts in this relational way.

Visual techniques are excellent for recalling, organising and summarising ideas. They are great for note-taking, problem-solving, report-writing, presentations and process-mapping.

Metaphorical

> We need to understand something of the casual structure of the world. (Steven Pinker – Professor of Psychology at Harvard University)

Because the modern world has grown away from the primitive intuitions about it, we have to invent devices to help us understand it. Analogies and metaphors are powerful ways of doing this. You will have spotted some of the following subjects being used as metaphors:

■ health, *food, *machines, *branching tree, *computing/internet, chaos theory, etc.

You can invent your own. This can be very useful for provoking and eliciting ideas.

Case study

A managing director of a company was trying to communicate the importance of customer focus, teamwork, financial results and safety during a board meeting. Because safety was in danger of becoming the 'poor relation' of the four, he used the analogy of juggling the fourth ball – it was difficult but the trick had to work. The analogy proved to be a potent tool. Even the chairman, addressing the board meeting, mimed a juggle as he spoke about the importance of safety.

Your circles of concern and influence

Stephen Covey writes in his book *The Seven Habits of Highly Effective People* that we all have common areas of our life. He talks about 'Circles of Influence' and 'Circles of Concern.' He suggests that we can influence what we achieve by what we say, and how we say it. A way to determine which area of concern that we are in is to distinguish between the 'have's' and 'be's':

- 'I'll be happy when I have my mortgage paid off.'
- 'If only I had a boss who wasn't such a dictator ...'
- 'If only I had a more patient husband ...'
- 'If only I had more obedient kids ...'
- 'If I had my degree ...'
- 'If I could just have more time to myself ...'

The circle of influence is filled with the be's – I can be more patient, be wise, be loving. It's the character focus. On any occasion when we think the problem is 'out there', that thought is our problem. We empower what's out there to control us. The change paradigm is 'outside-in' – what's out there has to change before we can change.

The proactive approach is to change from the inside-out: to be different, by being different, to effect positive change in what's out there – I can be more resourceful, I can be more diligent, I can be more creative, I can be more co-operative.

One of Stephen's favourite stories is from the Old Testament. It's the story of Joseph, who was sold into slavery in Egypt by his brothers at the age of 17. Can you imagine how easy it would have been for him to languish in self-pity as a servant of Potiphar, to focus on the weaknesses of his brothers and his captors and on all he didn't have? But Joseph was proactive. He worked hard, and within a short time was running Potiphar's household. He was in charge of all that Potiphar had because Potiphar trusted him. Then came the day when Joseph was caught in a difficult situation and refused to compromise his integrity. As a result, he was unjustly imprisoned for 13 years. But again he was proactive. He worked on the inner circle, on being instead of having, and soon he was running the prison and eventually the entire nation of Egypt, second only to the Pharaoh.

I know that this idea involves a dramatic paradigm shift for many people. It is so much easier to blame other people, conditioning, or conditions for our own stagnant situation. But we are responsible – 'responsible' – to control our lives and to have a powerful influence on our circumstances by working on being, on what we are.

If I have a problem with my marriage, what do I gain by continually confessing my wife's sins? By saying I'm not responsible, I make myself a powerless victim; I immobilise myself in a negative situation, and I also diminish my ability to influence her – my nagging, accusing, critical attitude only makes her feel validated in her own weakness. My criticism is worse than the conduct I want to correct. My ability to impact the situation positively will wither and die.

If I really want to improve my situation, I can work on the one thing over which I have control – myself. I can stop trying to change my wife and work on my own weaknesses. I can focus on being a great marriage partner, a source of unconditional love and support. I hope my wife will feel the power of the proactive example and respond in kind. But whether she does or doesn't, the most positive way I can influence my situation is to work on myself, on my being.

There are many ways to work in the Circle of Influence – to be a better listener, to be a more loving marriage partner, to be a better student, to be a more co-operative and dedicated employee. Sometimes the most proactive thing you can do is to be happy, just to genuinely smile. Happiness, like unhappiness, is a proactive choice. There are things, such as the weather, that our circle of influence will never include. But as proactive people we can carry our own physical or social weather with us. We can be happy and accept those things that at present we can't control, while we focus our efforts on the things we can.

How to become more creative

Everybody has the ability to become more creative in their everyday activities. For most, we are what we are and there are certain aspects of our personalities that we cannot change. However, we can practise new skills and we can enhance our repertoire. It seems that there are four factors, above all, that are required for us to become a more creative thinker.

1. A tremendous amount of information – memory sharpened by practice and positive feedback.

2. A willingness to generate ideas – for fun and enjoyment.

3. A large waste bin – you must be willing to evaluate and discriminate between junk and good ideas.

4. A surplus of energy and attention – you must be willing to devote all your spare energy to your own area of interest.

There are several strategies to help improve creativity:

- use all of your brain – the logical side and the creative side;
- access the unconscious;
- reinstate the intuitive;
- loosen your concepts – use fluidity;
- develop a sense of curiosity – ask challenging questions;
- do things you enjoy – and enjoy things you do;
- immerse yourself in what you are good at.

Another key factor when developing your creative thinking is to consider when and where you might be most creative.

Creating the right environment

Archimedes did it in his bath. Newton found it under an apple tree. Where are you most creative? We can take our lead from others who are considered creative achievers. Top executives can get their inspiration in some surprising ways. Here are some of them (source: Roffey Park Management

Institute's Report – *Innovation at the Top*): the way that different essences make a perfume; the way a chef prepares food, care, attention to detail, quality; Zen philosophy; the harmony of music.

The perspective of senior managers is shaped by what they read, watch, listen to and experience in private. It is clear from the study that interests outside the workplace influence decision-making. The majority of the best ideas occurred away from the workplace in natural settings such as train or plane journeys, walking, relaxing, playing music. Sport and comedy seem to be featured highly. Here are some of the most mentioned stimuli:

- humour and wit on radio and TV;
- networking as a source of stimulus;
- talking to passengers on a train;
- conversation or contact with colleagues;
- 'dreaming or drifting' (this often happens in the oddest places: gardening, the opera, walking, etc., but can result in breakthrough ideas);
- the community and specialist groups for stimulus and support;
- reading – some find inspiration through a fictional character or historical personality;
- radio – stimulates imagination in a particular way;
- leisure – renew skills and enthusiasm;
- time alone for creative thought.

All achievers are creative in their own unique ways. A self-taught chef, Michael Bras, found inspiration and wild herbs while running in his native hills in the southern Auvergne. His specialism is wild and unusual plants. He says, 'I run several times a week in the mountains and it is from these runs that I harvest ideas and emotions.' He finds his inspiration from nature, and hopes to express through his food, 'a climate, freedom of expression, a sense of expression, a sense of wonderment, a joie de vivre'. He compares his cooking to jazz, 'for its architecture, its fluid elegance, its silences'.

A good night's sleep

Harvard Medical School claims that a consistent good sleep can make you 40% smarter. Sleep is crucial to memory foundation and learning. Sleep is not passive, it is active in the functioning of the brain. REM (rapid eye movement) sleep relates to the cortex of the brain, which is the storehouse of associative memory. It is good at processing context – just like certain aspects of creativity. Good sleep allows us to process facts and perceptions and build them into coherent patterns. The challenge today is that many think they are too busy to get the right amount of sleep. If we are right about the critical role of the unconscious in creative thought, then the role of sleep and deep relaxation may need to be re-evaluated.

Creative people engineer the right time, place and conditions for productive thought.

Changing the box

- Being unique – stealing a business advantage by being different from the rest

For all intents and purposes, you are the box that you live in. Most of us make self-limiting assumptions about the nature of our world. However, there are great opportunities to create connections between different parts of our lives, and in turn have a distinct advantage over others who only see the world from a two-dimensional point of view. Why is it important to understand the need to keep changing the box we live and work in? 'Thinking outside the box' ensures that you keep your thinking fresh and different from everyone else, and we can then say to our team members and customers, 'Come to us, we are not like all the others.'

We have to be open-minded, ahead of the game, one step ahead, because our customers expect more and more. We as customers are exactly the same, we expect more and more. The greatest limit on possible achievement is an invisible, self-limiting 'box' we draw around us and our business. Below is an old puzzle: all you have to do is join all nine dots with four straight lines without the pen leaving the paper.

. . .

. . .

. . .

If you think outside the confines of the nine dots, the puzzle is easily solved; however, one nine-year-old girl said she could do it in one, and her answer is illustrated below.

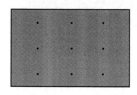

Many adults express shock, or even slight anger at this solution. Surely she had cheated? But it is worth remembering that one person's innovation is another's cheating. All she had to do was redefine the opportunity. Most people attempting the puzzle set themselves the self-limiting barrier that a line is thin and the dots are far apart.

It should be considered that the kind of thinking that creates a one-line solution is normally open, fresh and even childlike in its simplicity.

Why not start realigning your thinking by:

- redefining the expectations of your business;
- focusing on the potential rather than the expected;
- allowing your customers to help you change the shape of your box;
- encouraging the team to help you change your box;
- stealing/borrowing from other people's boxes;
- learning from other industries;
- considering *everything*!

A key technique to help your overall effectiveness

There are some fundamental principles to help you become more effective in your daily routines. Stephen Covey outlines the following key concept in his book *The Seven Habits of Highly Effective People*. He says that principles become the basis of a person's character, creating an empowering centre of correct maps from which an individual can effectively solve problems, maximise opportunities, and continually learn and integrate other principles in an upward spiral of growth.

Habit of effectiveness

Some principles can become habits of effectiveness because they are based on a paradigm of effectiveness that is in harmony with a natural law, a principle called 'P/PC balance' (see further overleaf), which many people break themselves against. The principle can be easily understood by remembering Aesop's fable of the goose and the golden egg.

The fable is the story of a poor farmer who discovers in the nest of his pet goose a glittering golden egg. At first, he thinks it must be some kind of trick. But as he starts to throw the egg aside, he has second thoughts and takes it to be appraised instead. The egg is pure gold! The farmer can't believe his luck. He becomes more incredulous the next morning when the experience is repeated. Day after day, he awakens to rush to the nest and find another golden egg. He becomes fabulously wealthy; it seems too good to be true.

But with his increasing wealth comes greed and impatience. Unable to wait day after day for the golden eggs, the farmer decides he will kill the goose and get them all at once. But when he opens the goose, he finds it empty. There are no more golden eggs – and now there is no way to get any more. The farmer had destroyed the goose that produced them.

Within this fable is a natural law, a principle – the basic definition of effectiveness. Most people see effectiveness from the golden egg paradigm: the more you produce, the more you do, the more effective you are. But as the story shows, true effectiveness is a function of two things: what is produced (the golden eggs) and the producing asset or capacity to produce (the goose).

If you adopt a pattern of life that focuses on golden eggs and neglects the goose, you will soon be without the asset that produces golden eggs. On the other hand, if you only take care of the goose and neglect the golden eggs, you will soon not be able to feed yourself or the goose.

The balanced approach

Effectiveness lies in the balance – the 'P/PC balance.' P stands for Production of desired results, the golden eggs. PC stands for Production Capability, the ability or asset that produces the golden eggs.

Mind-mapping

Do you have a reliable method of retaining information and thinking in a creative manner? There is no limit to what you can retain and develop in your mind. The key secrets are imagination and association.

> Realise that in some way everything connects to everything else. (Leonardo da Vinci)

By using your imagination, you are thinking like a child, and children have *vivid* imaginations. Tony Buzan, the mind-mapping guru, says that 'a picture is worth a thousand words' and Einstein once wrote 'imagination is more important than knowledge.'

I recently attended a mind-mapping workshop run by Tony. He explained that people's lack of information retention was a result of a number of factors, e.g. little focus on certain topics in the first place, lack of priority or simply an overall feeling of indifference.

Adopt a new technique, for example with star signs:

- Capricorn (Dec. 22 – Jan. 20): unicorn, first month, thirsty animal
- Aquarius (Jan. 21 – Feb. 19): water, drinking at side of a river
- Pisces (Feb. 20 – Mar. 20): fish, inside the river are fish
- Aries (Mar. 21 – Apr. 20): goat, being watched by a goat

- Taurus (Apr. 21 – May 21): bull, standing in a field next to a bull
- Gemini (May 22 – Jun. 21): twins, not one bull but twins
- Cancer (Jun. 22 – Jul. 23): crab, twins have two arms, two legs and crabs two claws
- Leo (Jul. 24 – Aug. 23): lion, has claws too!
- Virgo (Aug. 24 – Sep. 23): maiden, lion's fab mane, maiden's fab dress
- Libra (Sep. 24 – Oct. 23): scales, lion and maiden go on scales and balance
- Scorpio (Oct. 24 – Nov. 22): scorpion, maiden's tattoo of scorpion on leg
- Sagittarius (Nov. 23 – Dec. 21): archer, aims his bow at the scorpion

Using your brain to the maximum

Self-awareness empowers us to examine our thoughts. This is particularly helpful in creating a personal mission statement because the two unique human endowments that enable us to practise imagination and conscience are primarily functions of the right side of the brain. Understanding how to tap into that right brain capacity greatly increases our creativity ability. Essentially, the left side of the brain is logical and verbal whereas the right is more intuitive and creative. The left deals with analysis, which means to pull apart; the right with synthesis, which means to put together. The left brain is time-bound, the right is time-free. Different people tend to use their dominant hemisphere and process every situation according to their right or left brain preference. Abraham Maslow (a prominent management scientist in the 1940s and 1950s who studied psychology) has a quotation that describes this process: 'He that is good with a hammer tends to think that everything is a nail.' The right brain and left brain people tend to look at things in different ways. We live in a primarily left-brain-dominant world, where words and measurement and logic are enthroned, and the more creative, intuitive, sensing, artistic aspect of our nature is used much less. Many find it difficult to tap into our right brain capacity.

Below are two suggestions to help tap into the right brain.

Expand perspective

Sometimes we are knocked out of our left brain thinking by an unplanned experience, e.g. a death of a loved one, a severe illness or a financial setback. This causes us to stand back and take a close look at our lives, and ask hard questions, e.g. What's really important? Why am I doing what I am doing? But you don't have to wait for certain circumstances to create experiences that expand your perspective. You can consciously create your own by using your imagination: visualise your own funeral (it has to be considered at some point), write your own eulogy, actually write it out, and be very specific. What do you want to be remembered for? How are you going to live your life in order to achieve this?

Visualisation and affirmation

A good affirmation has five basic ingredients: it's personal, it's positive, it's present tense, it's visual and it's emotional. For example: it's deeply satisfying (emotional) that I (personal) respond (present tense) with wisdom, respect, firmness and self-control (positive) when a member of my team makes a mistake.

Then you can visualise it. You can think about situations at work, and instead of seeing yourself getting upset, visualise yourself being able to handle the situation with respect and self-control that is captured by the affirmation above. If you practise this technique for all your affirmations (positive changes) then gradually your behaviour will change.

Instead of living out of the scripts given to you by your parents, society, genetics or your environment, you will be living out of the script that you have written from your own self-selected value system.

Dr Charles Garfield (Professor of Psychology at California University of Medicine, San Francisco) has researched peak performers from the fields of athletics and business. His research has shown that almost all peak performers are visualisers. They see it, they feel it, they experience it, before they actually do it. They begin with the end in mind. You can do this also.

Before a presentation, a difficult situation or confrontation, a meeting or meeting a specific goal, see it clearly, vividly, relentlessly and repeatedly. Create an internal 'comfort zone' so that when you arrive at the situation, it isn't foreign and it doesn't scare you.

Finding your service heart

Some successful businesses say that one of their key secrets to success is their reputation for service. This is achieved by recruiting agreeable and friendly people. Customers receive great service as a normal part of their service experience and this is delivered by people with personality, doing a job that they love (by and large).

Ken McCulloch, founder of Malmaison Hotels, puts four questions to new recruits:

- Do you understand what we are trying to do here?
- Can you deliver it? How? When?

He has high aspirations and these are backed up with fanatical attention to detail. Every employee has a pocket card that sets out how to achieve 'legendary service' with the customers. It reads:

- take responsibility and be enthusiastic;
- know your subject(s);
- be immaculate and be positive;
- prepare for service (maison place);
- communicate with each other;
- be yourself and enjoy yourself.

There is much controversial debate about how can we deliver great service every time. The answer is not in short sharp training courses (unfortunately for me) but in the heads of the service providers (management and staff). To relate better and to look after customers, the first essential relationship to create is with yourself. The most precise way of understanding the truth is that empathy comes from within.

Make a positive impression with your customers by boosting their overall customer experience. This can be achieved by:

- enhancing self-esteem, i.e. the customer is made to feel important in the eyes of the service provider;
- reduced anxiety, i.e. fears and concerns are identified, articulated and communicated by the behaviour of the service provider;

- increased self-confidence, i.e. the customer is made to feel proficient in use of equipment, knowledgeable in understanding of advice given by the service provider;

- comfort, i.e. the customer is made to feel physically and mentally at ease by the caring ambience and behaviour of the service provider;

- social status, i.e. the customer is made to believe that product/service will enhance his or her social status;

- reassurance, i.e. the customer is convinced that the decision to buy goods or service is the right one.

Bibliography

Adair, John (2002) *Effective Leadership*. London: Pan Books.

Barlow, Nigel May (2001) *Batteries Included*. London: Random House.

Butler, Gillian and Hope, Tony (1995) *Manage Your Mind*. Oxford: Oxford University Press.

Buzan, Tony (1991) *Use Both Sides of Your Brain*. New York: E.P. Dutton.

Carnegie, Dale (1982) *How to Win Friends and Influence People*. New York: Pocket Books.

Covey, Stephen (1989) *The Seven Habits of Highly Successful People*. London: Simon & Schuster.

Csikszentmihalyi, Mihaly (1991) *Flow – The Psychology of Optimal Experience*. New York: Harper Collins.

Galloway, Joe (2003) *Becoming a Category of One*. Chichester: John Wiley & Sons.

Harvey-Jones, Sir John (1988) *Making It Happen, Reflection on Leadership*. London: Collins.

Heppell, Michael (2004) *How to Be Brilliant*. London: Pearson Education.

Hucksley, Laura Archera (1963) *You Are Not the Target*. New York: Farrar, Straus.

Kundtz, David (1999) *Stopping*. Dublin: Newleaf.

Leigh, Andrew and Maynard, Michael (2002) *Leading Your Team*. London: Nicholas Brealey.

Lively, Lynn (1999) *The Procrastinator's Guide to Success*. New York: McGraw-Hill.

Loehr, James (2003) *The Power of Full Engagement*. London: Simon & Schuster.

McKenna, Paul (2004) *Change Your Life in 7 Days*. London: Bantam Press.

Milo, O. Frank (1987) *How to Get Your Point Across in 30 Seconds or Less*. London: Corgi Books.

Murphy, Joseph (1995) *The Power of Your Subconscious Mind*. New York: Pocket Books.

Rechtschaffen, Stephan (1997) *Timeshifting*. London: Doubleday.

Reeves, Richard (2001) *Happy Mondays*. London: Pearson Education.

Tricker, Bob (2003) *Essential Director*. London: Profile Books.

Whitmore, John (1992) *Coaching for Performance*. London: Nicholas Brealey.

Index